CONTENTS

INTRODUCTION

Many people question if Satan is real and whether he is responsible for evil in the world. Yet the Bible is clear that Satan exists and influences world events. Despite this, pastors are reluctant to preach sermons about Satan and his methods. Instead, many pastors prefer to preach positive sermons about Jesus because their congregations expect these types of sermons.

Although Jesus's atonement for our sins restored our relationship with God the Father, Christians are at war with an enemy that takes no prisoners. Satan is that enemy, and he is attacking Christians by any means necessary. Satan attacks Christians through deception and with oppressive spirits. These oppressive spirits torment Christians based on their hidden sins or generational curses, whereas nonbelievers are tormented because of their occult activities and sinful lifestyles.

Jesus's sacrifice for our sins gave us authority over Satan and his demons; however, Christians must be taught how to use this authority. This requires a knowledge of Scripture and how to apply it. In short, knowing how biblical verses apply to given situations. Also, one must have the boldness to confront demonic spirits. This can only occur if Christians are indwelled by the Holy Spirit.

Many Christians do not understand the purpose of the Holy Spirit. The Holy Spirit is not some mysterious force in the universe. Instead, it's the third person of the Trinity. Although we pray in Jesus's name to cast out demons, it's the power of the Holy Spirit that delivers us. Likewise, the inner voice of the Holy Spirit guides us daily. So to experience the full blessing and power of the Holy Spirit, one must surrender to him in mind, body, and spirit.

Full surrender to the Holy Spirit is necessary to fight the snares of the devil because only He can prepare Christians for spiritual warfare. Given this, Christians cannot be apathetic to the signs of the times. So every truly saved Christian must be empowered by the Holy Spirit to confront demonic spirits. This is necessary because God expects his children to do his will. One aspect of that will is to exercise authority over Satan and his demons.

Chapter 1

Evil

In 1973, *The Exorcist* was released. This movie depicts how a teenage girl becomes possessed and the subsequent exorcism by a Catholic priest to remove her demons. This exorcism has an eerie dialogue between these demons and the priest. In addition, there are many demonic manifestations to frighten the priest during this exorcism. Despite this, in the end, the girl gets delivered.

Although this was Hollywood, it was based on a real case that occurred in Saint Louis. Even though the movie fabricated some events from the original story, a full manifestation of demonic possession will show signs as portrayed in this movie. By today's horror movie standards, *The Exorcist* is slow-moving and not scary. Yet this movie deeply affected people in the seventies.

I watched this movie in 1973. Although I knew every demonic scene in the movie because of feedback from other teens, I felt real fear after watching it. The fear I felt was not based on religious beliefs because I was neither a Christian nor did I have preconceived ideas about demonic possession. Still, I felt this girl's demonic possession could happen to anyone. Despite this revelation, I was not convinced to start attending church or finding out more information about demonic possession.

When *The Exorcist* was released in 1973, the country was undergoing many societal changes. For instance, the traditional family unit was changing because of no-fault divorce. As a result, many Americans' attitudes about divorce changed. In addition, traditional Christian beliefs were under assault by the New Age movement. While on the political front, the Vietnam War was ending. Despite this, many Americans now held negative views about military service and the value of going to war.

In many ways, the changes that occurred in the country in 1973 set the table for the entire decade. And unlike the chaos of the 1960s, people in the 1970s became apathetic about their government, military, and religious faith. Yet for a short period, many Americans were moved after watching *The Exorcist*. They were moved because the Exorcist brought to light evil. As a result, people were shaken.

No one in Hollywood thought *The Exorcist* would be a box-office success. So when the movie brought in millions of dollars, movie executives were eager to produce more devil movies. However, the spin-offs to *The Exorcist* were not successful. They were not successful because the public wanted more horror than just scary music and flying objects. Once Hollywood figured this out, the new horror movies emphasized deranged killers and evil creatures that could not be killed.

This extreme effect changed how horror movies were made. As a result, plots for horror movies no longer matter. What mattered was the fearful effect on the audience. Because of this, today's horror movies have perfected the fear effect. In addition, horror movies are now violent and bloody. As a result, moviegoers are scared throughout these movies and can never relax while watching them. **Despite this, these horror movies continue to be popular.**

This fear effect within these movies can change people emotionally and spiritually. If it does, they will start engaging in dark activities that will change how they think, act, and believe. This is not a state that occurs overnight after watching one horror movie. Instead, this is a pattern of behavior that steadily gets worse. Sadly, often this strange behavior over time can be an early sign of demonic possession.

Few would argue that horror movies since 1973 have negatively affected people. And sometimes, this negative effect changes people spiritually. Still, detecting the physical signs of those afflicted by demons can be difficult. It can be difficult because unlike what is shown in horror movies, true demonic attacks are deceptive and hidden from others. So those not affected by demonic entities won't see or feel what tormented individuals experience.

Many times tormented individuals get diagnosed with psychiatric problems and are prescribed mind-numbing medications. Likewise, if the affliction is severe enough, individuals can be sent to mental institutions even though their problem is not mental illness—it's demonic possession. Given this, the use of mind-controlling drugs is the devil's plan to keep people suppressed spiritually.

Although horror films can open doors to demonic oppression, the greatest effect of these films is deception. Satan is the master of deception. He plans his deception in ways we do not understand. For instance, *The Exorcist* movie deceived people about demonic oppression and possession. Hence, because of this movie, people expect to see signs as portrayed in The *Exorcist* when a person is possessed or oppressed. So if people cannot see the physical signs as portrayed in horror movies, they cannot recognize demonic affliction. As a result, people who are truly oppressed by demonic spirits are never delivered. Sadly, they use alcohol or drugs to cope if they don't get delivered. In extreme cases, some commit suicide to escape their torment.

Satan wants us to believe his attacks against people are mental, not spiritual. This is Satan's tactic to keep people from getting delivered. Since Satan knows true deliverance can only occur after an individual accepts Christ and is filled with the Holy Spirit. We find verses in the Bible that outline Satan's tactics and plans. In Ephesians 6:12, Paul describes the nature of Satan and his dark influences on us: **"For we do not wrestle against flesh and blood, but against principalities, against powers, against the rulers of the darkness of this age, against spiritual hosts of wickedness in the heavenly places."** Given this passage, we must understand our fight is spiritual, not physical. Thus, Satan and his demons must be fought with the weapons of the spirit.

Possession versus Oppression

People have preconceived ideas about demonic possession and oppression. Sadly, people formed these views based on horror films. Yet the depiction of demonic forces in movies is sensationalized. So these films do not accurately portray how possessed individuals are affected. One point, though, that is accurate in horror movies is how demons slowly take control of individuals. This is not a state that occurs overnight.

Instead, this is a sequence of events that break down individuals mentally and spiritually. So oppressed individuals don't lose control of their minds and spirit. Instead, they have stretches when dark spirits influence what they say, do, and think. Dark spirits often oppress Christians this way because they cannot possess them. They cannot possess Christians because Satan and his demons need spiritual permission to torment a person. They torment individuals in two ways: possession (total control of a person) or oppression (periods of control and manipulation of a person). Still, Satan must have a reason and justification to attack one. His reasons could be based on one's sins or that of their bloodline.

Bloodline curses are your family's history of sin. This is either a known or unknown sin. Conditions such as alcoholism, drug addiction, pornography, and violent behavior are common generational curses that get passed down. Although some believe these problems are learned behaviors, they are not. Instead, the core reason for these conditions is spiritual. Despite this, a person who gives their life to Christ can break their family's generational curse. Yet to break the generational curses of one's bloodline, one must first acknowledge them. Unfortunately, many generational curses within Christian families are unknown. As a result, these generational curses are never broken. As a result, they get passed down to the next generation.

A generational curse is an example of how oppressive spirits torment Christians. In contrast, generational curses for nonbelievers can lead to demonic possession. Mainly because they do not have the Holy Spirit residing within them, which is a gift from God after accepting Christ. Despite this, Satan cannot arbitrarily possess a person. He must have a spiritual legal right to do so. Given this, nonbelievers can fight off demonic possession, but to do so, nonbelievers must stay away from occult activities that allow the devil in.

Nonbelievers can cry out to God for deliverance from oppressive spirits, but they must recognize the attacks of the devil. Also, the only way for nonbelievers to be delivered from demonic attacks is to accept Christ as Savior. Unfortunately, if the devil possesses a nonbeliever, he will hinder them from crying out to God. Therefore, it's crucial to recognize the signs of demonic oppression versus possession of self and others.

Few Christians contemplate demonic oppression or possession. Likewise, few pastors preach on the subject. Yet most Christians know

Satan and his demons are responsible for much of the evil in the world. In addition, most believers acknowledge things are not getting better in the world. Despite this, the church refuses to address demonic activity in the world and implement strategies to confront it. In many ways, Christians know facts about Satan, but they don't understand the depths of his power and influence in the world. Conversely, Jesus understood Satan's authority in the world; however, Jesus's death on the cross broke Satan's authority over us.

One of the strongest passages in the Bible concerning demonic possession can be found in Mark 5:1–12: **Then they came to the other side of the sea, to the country of the Gadarenes. And when He had come out of the boat, immediately there met Him out of the tombs a man with an unclean spirit, who had his dwelling among the tombs; and no one could bind him, not even with chains, because he had often been bound with shackles and chains. And the chains had been pulled apart by him, and the shackles broken in pieces; neither could anyone tame him. And always, night and day, he was in the mountains and in the tombs, crying out and cutting himself with stones. When he saw Jesus from afar, he ran and worshipped Him. And he cried out with a loud voice and said, "What have I to do with You, Jesus, Son of the Most High God? I implore You by God that You do not torment Me." For He said to him, "Come out of the man, unclean spirit!" Then He asked him, "What is your name?" And he answered, saying, "My name is Legion; for we are many." Also he begged Him earnestly that He would not send them out of the country. Now a large herd of swine was feeding there near the mountains. So all the demons begged Him, saying, "Send us to the swine, that we may enter them."**

Several points within these verses describe the authority and attributes of demons. The first point is that demons are assigned to areas of responsibility. In this passage, the demons were dwelling among the tombs. Further, the demons begged Jesus not to cast them out of the country. So even though Jesus allowed these demons to enter a herd of swine, they did not leave the area—just the man. Also, Jesus had the power to deliver people from demonic possession. In contrast, many clergymen today do not believe demonic spirits can oppress Christians. Yet Scripture is clear the devil can oppress people—even Christians.

These verses also confirm that possessed individuals can perform supernatural feats. The possessed man in this story broke apart chains and shackles. Chains and shackles in the first century were thick and made from iron. Yet this tormented man could break apart chains and shackles. In addition, the phrase "could not be tamed" refers to his behavior and dark disposition. No doubt the townspeople feared this man. Yet there is no mention the townspeople tried to kill him. No doubt the townspeople could not kill him because of the demonic power inside him. This is an important point to ponder since demonically possessed individuals cannot be cured with counseling sessions or medication. Instead, the only cure for removing demonic forces from individuals is a Christian deliverance.

Jesus also confirmed in this passage that demons are individuals, not mindless evil spirits floating around. So Jesus told the demonic spirits to identify themselves. Jesus knew to deliver a person from a dark spirit the identity of the dark entity must be known. Once the demon is known, one must speak to that entity. For example, one would demand that the demon of unforgiveness, bitterness, addiction, or anger be removed in Jesus's name. So even if the tormenting demon is unclear, one demands the demon responsible be removed from the individual.

Once an individual has been delivered from demonic control, they must address the factors that caused it. If not, the demons will come back stronger. Therefore, the delivered individual must accept Christ and allow the Holy Spirit to fill them up spiritually. This is crucial because the Bible confirms that demons that have been exorcized can return. We find this in Matthew 12:43–45:

> **"When an unclean spirit goes out of a man, he goes through dry places, seeking rest, and finds none. Then he says, 'I will return to my house from which I came.' And when he comes, he finds it empty, swept, and put in order. Then he goes and takes with him seven other spirits more wicked than himself, and they enter and dwell there; and the last state of that man is worse than the first. So shall it also be with this wicked generation."**

Given this passage, it's critical once an individual has been delivered from demonic control that they keep their mental and spiritual guard up.

We find another example in the Bible that describes the actions of one possessed. This passage can be found in Mark 9:17–27: **Then one of the crowd answered and said, "Teacher, I brought You my son, who has a mute spirit. "And wherever it seizes him, it throws him down; he foams at the mouth, gnashes his teeth, and becomes rigid. So I spoke to Your disciples, that they should cast it out, but they could not." He answered him and said, "O faithless generation, how long shall I be with you? How long shall I bear with you? Bring him to Me." Then they brought him to Him. And when he saw Him, immediately the spirit convulsed him, and he fell on the ground and wallowed, foaming at the mouth. So He asked his father, "How long has this been happening to him?" And he said, "From childhood. And often he has thrown him both into the fire and into the water to destroy him. But if You can do anything, have compassion on us and help us." Jesus said to him, "If you can believe, all things are possible to him who believes." Immediately the father of the child cried out and said with tears, "Lord, I believe; help my unbelief!" When Jesus saw that the people came running together, He rebuked the unclean spirit, saying to it: "Deaf and dumb spirit, I command you, come out of him and enter him no more!" Then the spirit cried out, convulsed him greatly, and came out of him. And he became as one dead, so that many said, "He is dead." But Jesus took him by the hand and lifted him up, and he arose.**

These verses confirm a possessed person will exhibit physical signs such as foaming from the mouth, shaking, and wild behavior that is not natural. Given this, routine mental health treatment cannot help those who are possessed because they are not experiencing physical ailments or psychological breakdowns. Instead, they are under demonic control from evil entities. Given this, when one is under demonic control, the demons within must be ordered to leave an individual. This is done by performing a Christian deliverance. A Christian deliverance is like what Jesus did to expel the mute spirit from the boy. The only difference is how long the deliverance might take. A Christian deliverance could take hours.

Although all Christians have the authority to expel demons from individuals and themselves, many believers do not have the faith and boldness to confront demonic spirits. In addition, the spiritual principle of gifting comes into play. In short, what are your spiritual gifts. Thus, if you have not been called to discern dark spirits and have the boldness to confront them, it's not your lane to confront possessed individuals. We find in Jude 1:9 confirmation of spiritual lanes of responsibility: **Yet Michael the archangel, in contending with the devil, when he disputed about the body of Moses, dared not bring against him a reviling accusation, but said, "The Lord rebuke you!"** If an archangel felt he could not chastise the devil, we must be careful in how we confront the devil too. Therefore, we must learn how to depend on the inner voice of the Holy Spirit when dealing with demonic situations.

Halloween

Another demonic deception within our culture involves the celebration of Halloween. For decades, many people viewed Halloween as a holiday for kids. This holiday was second only to Christmas for most children. On a personal note, some of my best memories as a child occurred on Halloween night. I never felt fear during Halloween, nor did I think my parents needed to accompany me while trick or treating. Granted, this was during the sixties and seventies, but the thought of something bad happening to me never crossed my mind.

I still vividly remember my Halloween experience when I was eight. Sadly, no child today would ever go trick or treating at eight unaccompanied. Although Halloween is still a major holiday for children today, many parents won't allow their kids to participate due to security concerns. In addition, many Christians won't celebrate Halloween because of its origin.

Many people know that Halloween was a pagan holiday that predated Christianity. Many of the beliefs and mythology of Halloween started with the Celtic festival of Samhain, which was practiced in ancient Britain. This festival was established because pagans believed that on October 31, the dead revisited their homes. Because of this belief, the practice of wearing masks, and putting on costumes to scare away the dead was born. Likewise, the folklore of witches, demons, and goblins began. As time passed, though, this holiday took on mythological qualities that remain today. For example, the belief in good fortune from the devil became popular. Given this, many believed that good health, luck, and successful marriages could be obtained during this festival period. Thus, in many ways, the pagans of ancient Britain were practicing devil worshiping.

Halloween as we know it today always had images of ghosts, goblins, and witches. Yet these mythical characters were not always viewed as evil. For example, Casper the friendly ghost was a popular persona that many people viewed positively as someone who died and came back to do good--even though it was a cartoon for kids. Likewise, television shows in the 1960s and 1970s presented witches as individuals who wanted to do good, not evil.

The release of *The Exorcist* and the subsequent devil horror movies changed our perception of ghosts, goblins, and witches. As a result, these mythical characters were now considered evil servants of Satan. This perception extended to how we viewed Halloween too. As a result, Halloween was no longer viewed as a fun holiday for kids. So many Christian parents during the 1980s did not allow their children to go trick or treating. It was also during this period that churches started to offer alternative events for children on Halloween night. In contrast, though, many nonreligious adults started viewing Halloween as an opportunity to dress up and party.

To scare or be scared became a popular practice during the 1980s. To be scared and have a good time was the goal for parties on Halloween night. In addition, many people started to view Halloween night as a holiday like Thanksgiving or Christmas. Thereafter, the practice of decorating homes with scary Halloween displays became popular. I noticed this attitude change about decorating one's home for Halloween when I returned to the United States from Germany in 1993 after serving a six-year tour with the Army. I was assigned to a recruiting office in Alton, Illinois. I found that many homes in my recruiting zone were decorated for Halloween weeks before October 31. I found this odd considering that many of the people in my zone had limited incomes. So I could not understand why people would waste money on these displays. Because when I grew up, Halloween was never considered a major holiday-- just a fun night for kids. Yet something changed in the country about celebrating Halloween.

Another recent trend about Halloween that has gained popularity is haunted houses. Many people look forward to visiting these haunted houses leading up to Halloween. The goal is to be scared. This is especially true for teenagers. Even in small towns, firehouses are transformed into haunted houses for kids. Even parents with small children don't see anything wrong with exposing their children to scary things. In many ways, our spiritual senses surrounding Halloween have been deadened.

No doubt a powerful reason for this spiritual deadening is due to television. By any measure, television programming today is violent and sexually suggestive. Even nonbelievers admit that television has become violent and suggestive. As a result, because of television and other dark aspects of our culture, many Christians cannot discern Satan's demonic devices. One of those devices is exposing children to scary things during Halloween.

In many ways, Halloween has become a holiday Satan uses to erode our spiritual senses. This has occurred because the illusions and festivities surrounding Halloween can affect our spiritual discernment. The Celtics were right—this is a holiday of the dead—not the physically dead, but the spiritually dead. In 2 Corinthians 2:11, we are given a warning about Satan's ways: **Lest Satan should take advantage of us; for we are not ignorant of his devices**. Given this passage, Christians cannot avoid the dark aspects of Halloween. Also, there are spiritual consequences for children who participate in activities associated with Halloween. Therefore, Christians cannot participate in activities during Halloween that dishonor God and promote the devil's agenda.

Horoscopes and Psychics

Many people look forward to reading their daily horoscope. On the surface, this activity seems like harmless fun for most people. Yet some people believe daily horoscope predictions have merit. Although faith in horoscope predictions is not a doorway to the occult, it could be a demonic seed that is planted in one's mind. That seed is faith in the supernatural to get answers and gain an advantage over others. Often psychic readings can be the next step for those who believe in horoscopes. And unlike horoscopes, though, this is not a harmless step with no consequences. Furthermore, if the psychic is a true medium (an individual that calls upon demonic spirits) this action can lead to demonic oppression.

In the Bible, there is a famous story of King Saul, who sought out a medium because he feared an attack from the Philistine army. He feared the Philistine army because God abandoned him due to his disobedience. Likewise, his spiritual leader Samuel the prophet, had died. In 1 Samuel 28:5–16, we are told about Saul's mental state, and why he sought a medium:

When Saul saw the army of the Philistines, he was afraid, and his heart trembled greatly. And when Saul inquired of the Lord, the Lord did not answer him, either by dreams or by Urim or by the prophets. Then Saul said to his servants, "Find me a woman who is a medium, that I may go to her and inquire of her." And his servants said to him, "In fact, there is a woman who is a medium at En Dor." So Saul disguised himself and put on other clothes, and he went, and two men with him; and they came to the woman by night. And he said, "Please conduct a séance for me, and bring up me the one I shall name to you." Then the woman said to him, "Look, you know what Saul has done, how he has cut off the mediums and the spiritists from the land, Why then do you lay a snare for my life, to cause me to die?" And Saul swore to her by the Lord, saying, "As the Lord lives, no punishment shall come upon you for this thing." Then the woman said, "Whom shall I bring up for you?" And he said, "Bring up Samuel for me." When the woman saw Samuel, she cried out with a loud voice. And the woman spoke to Saul, saying, "Why have you deceived me? For you are Saul!" And the king said to her, "Do not be afraid. What did you see?" And the woman said to Saul, "I saw a spirit ascending out of the earth." So he said to her, "What is his form?" And she said, "An old man is coming up, and he is covered with a mantle." And Saul perceived that it was Samuel, and he stooped with his face to the ground and bowed down. Now Samuel said to Saul, "Why have you disturbed me by bringing me up?" And Saul answered, "I am deeply distressed; for the Philistines make war against me, and God has departed from me and does not answer me anymore, neither by prophets nor by dreams, Therefore I have called you, that you may reveal to me what I should do." Then Samuel said: "So why do you ask me, seeing the Lord has departed from you and has become your enemy?"

There are several spiritual points in these verses. The first point is that mediums can summon demonic spirits. Although these verses seem to indicate Samuel spoke to Saul, the Lord allowed this for his purposes. Despite this, there is no biblical tenet that supports the idea of dead people communicating with the living. There is a powerful story in the Bible that forbids interaction between the living and the dead. This is found in Luke 16:22–26:

> So it was that the beggar died, and was carried by the angels to Abraham's bosom. The rich man also died and was buried. "And being in torments in Hades, he lifted up his eyes and saw Abraham afar, and Lazarus in his bosom. "Then he cried and said, 'Father Abraham, have mercy on me, and send Lazarus that he may dip the tip of his finger in water and cool my tongue, for I am tormented in this flame.' But Abraham said, 'Son, remember that in your lifetime you received your good things, and likewise Lazarus evil things; but now he is comforted and you are tormented. And besides all this, between us and you there is a great gulf fixed, so that those who want to pass from here to you cannot, nor can those from there pass to us.'"

Although these verses contrast the comfort of Heaven compared to the torment of Hell, they also confirm individuals are forbidden from traveling between the two places. Hence, the people in Heaven cannot comfort those in Hell. Likewise, those in Hell cannot escape their torment-- even for a moment. This point is confirmed by the rich man begging Abraham to send Lazarus to his brothers, but Abraham says no. Instead, he tells the rich man his brothers have Moses and the prophets to learn about Hell. This comment refers to the biblical accounts of Moses and the prophets.

This passage also confirms that psychics are not bringing up deceived individuals. Instead, they are deceiving people who desperately want to communicate with deceased loved ones. So Christians should never attempt to use a psychic for any purpose. When they do so, they undermine Scripture and diminish the purpose of the Holy Spirit. It's the Holy Spirit that reveals the things of God to us. Even information about deceased loved ones—if that is God's will for us to know. Given this, psychics should never be considered God's servants, and Christians should never use them.

There are no Christian psychics. Instead, they are Satan's servants. Although television shows of psychics helping people are popular-- this is a deception. This is a deception because psychics are not receiving messages from departed loved ones, but from demonic spirits—assuming they are true mediums. The Bible tells us Satan and his demons can fool us. In 2 Corinthians 11:14–15, we find two verses that outline this deception: **And no wonder! Satan himself transforms himself into an angel of light. Therefore it is no great thing if his ministers also transform themselves into ministers of righteous, whose end will be according to their works.** Given this passage, accurate information revealed by psychics does not prove deceased loved ones conveyed it. What it does prove is that oppressive spirits have established a foothold within one's family's bloodline.

In the Bible, we are told that every word we speak and the things we do are recorded. God and Satan are recording our actions but for different purposes. This pertains to everyone, not just Christians. So nothing we do in thought or action is hidden from God because he is omnipresent and omniscient. The devil also uses information about us to oppress us. A lot of this information about us is passed down to the devil because of family generational curses.

Many families have generational curses such as alcoholism, drug addiction, gambling, or anger that have been passed down through generations. Once curses have been established within a family's bloodline, demons are assigned to its members. As a result, demons have observed all the events family members have done through the years. As a result, they can convey messages via psychics to you about your past and that of your loved ones.

The good news is that most psychics are frauds. Nevertheless, many psychics are skilled at reading body language. This enables them to probe you with questions that appear insightful. For instance, they may ask: have you recently suffered a loss or disappointment? How you respond will determine their next series of questions. This is the same technique that salespeople use. On a personal note, I used this technique when I worked as an Army recruiter in the nineties.

This sales technique is known as probing. For example, I would never ask recruits about joining the army. Instead, I would ask how they felt about the military. Then based on their responses, I would tailor my questions to get an interview with them. Thus, once I spoke to recruits face-to-face, many of their objections about joining the army could be answered. I also discovered that my personality played a role in convincing recruits to join the army. Likewise, many psychics are effective communicators too, and they use this skill to con people.

Unlike salesmen trying to sell you products, pursuing answers to your problems through psychics has spiritual consequences even if the psychic is a fraud. The reason: You're seeking guidance from demonic sources instead of from God. Christians can never seek out psychics for answers. Also, if nonbelievers pursue psychics for answers, they will harden their hearts to the Holy Spirit. Once a nonbeliever hardens their heart to the Holy Spirit, they may never get another invitation to accept Christ.

The Bible tells us it's the Father that draws people to the Son through the Holy Spirit. Given this, people cannot seek answers for their sorrows through the occult. When they do so, these actions will close out God. Although God is love, patience, and long-suffering he cannot tolerate idolatry—faith in anything other than him. There are many verses in the Bible warning us about idolatry and putting our faith in other things besides God. We find in Deuteronomy 18:10–12 a clear warning from God to stay away from the things of the occult: **There shall not be found among you anyone who makes his son or his daughter pass through the fire, or one who practices witchcraft, or a soothsayer, or one who interprets omens, or a sorcerer, or one who conjures spells, or a medium, or a spiritist, or one who calls up the dead. For all who do these things are an abomination to the Lord, and because of these abominations the Lord your God drives them out from before you.**

This warning was given to the Israelites, but it applies to Christians too. Furthermore, there are serious spiritual consequences for Christians who engage in these types of activities. The worst consequence is losing their fellowship with God. Granted, a Christian's spirit is born-again, but their body, mind, and will are not. So Christians must attend church regularly, read their Bibles often, and pray without ceasing. To pray without ceasing means one has a spiritual mindset that governs how they live.

Constant communication through prayer with God is the key. This is not mindless chanting prayers all day. Instead, it's an awareness of God's presence via the Holy Spirit inside you. The Holy Spirit's job is to warn, reveal, and guide you daily. For the Holy Spirit to do his job, you must be willing to hear his voice. You acknowledge him by listening to his urges and praying about everything. The Holy Spirit may direct you when to pray on matters or proclaim victory over spiritual strongholds. Given how special the Holy Spirit is to Christians, God won't tolerate believers that reject his guidance. When Christians do so, God's hedge of protection against demonic forces can be taken away.

There are other warnings in the Bible about idolatry. For instance, the Second Commandment warns us not to have idols. Although this often refers to graven images that people worship or bow down to, it also applies to faith in anything other than God. Furthermore, in Exodus 20:5–6 another aspect of the Second Commandment warns us about generational curses: **You shall not bow down to them nor serve them. For I, the Lord your God, am a jealous God, visiting the iniquity of the fathers upon the children to the third and forth generations of those who hate Me, but showing mercy to thousands, to those who love Me and keep My commandments.** The curse here pertains to false Gods; however, it also applies to other grievous sins of the Father. Grievous sins are those committed against others and self but have psychological and spiritual consequences for family members. As a result, when fathers won't repent of these sins, they open the door to oppressive spirits against their families.

Generational Curses

Many pastors insist demons cannot torment Christians. They contend Jesus defeated Satan two thousand years ago when he died on the cross for our sins. This is a true statement; however, when Christians have lukewarm faith and live like nonbelievers, they lose their authority to confront demonic spirits. Because of this, carnal Christians (believers who live like non-believers) should never attempt to confront demons. If they do so, they won't be successful; moreover, they invite demonic consequences. A powerful illustration of this point can be found in Acts 19:13–16: **Then some of the itinerant Jewish exorcists took it upon themselves to call the name of the Lord Jesus over those who had evil spirits, saying, "We exorcise you by the Jesus whom Paul preaches." Also there were seven sons of Sceva, a Jewish chief priest, who did so. And the evil spirit answered and said, "Jesus I know, and Paul I know; but who are you?" Then the man in whom the evil spirit was leaped on them, overpowered them, and prevailed against them, so that they fled out of that house naked and wounded.**

Although these Jewish exorcists were not Christians, no doubt they knew how to expel demonic spirits from people. Yet we are not told in Scripture how successful they were before Jesus's resurrection. What is clear after Jesus's resurrection is that only spirit-filled Christians have the authority to expel demons. The reason: Jesus's death on the cross restored mankind's authority on earth. Thus, Christians are God's children and have access to his authority and power on earth. One part of that power is the authority over Satan and his demons. In Mark 16:17–18, Jesus tells his apostles the authority that believers have: **And these signs will follow those who believe: In My name they will cast out demons; they will speak with new tongues; they will take up serpents; and if they drink anything deadly, it will by no means hurt them; they will lay hands on the sick, and they will recover.**

Although some believe these verses only applied to the apostles, other biblical passages contend all believers have this authority and power. Many born-again Christians have experienced the signs as listed in Mark 16:17–18. Yet few have participated in or witnessed an exorcism. This is not unusual. Since exorcisms are usually performed within controlled environments by trained individuals. Christians not trained to conduct exorcisms should not be present during one. Chiefly because exorcisms are intense, and believers unprepared for them can be overwhelmed or attacked.

This is not a question of faith, but a question of calling. So if you are not called to conduct exorcisms, you should not attempt one. They should not attempt one because this type of spiritual warfare is different from just resisting the thoughts of the devil. We find proof of callings in the Bible. The strongest support for this can be found in 1 Corinthians 12:14–20. In these verses, Paul compares believers' gifts to body parts: **For in fact the body is not one member but many. If the foot should say, "Because I am not a hand, I am not of the body," is it therefore not of the body? And if the ear should say, "Because I am not an eye, I am not of the body," is it therefore not of the body? If the whole body were an eye, where would be the hearing? If the whole were hearing, where would be the smelling? But now God has set the members, each one of them, in the body just as He pleased. And if they were all one member, where would the body be? But now indeed there are many members, yet one body.** The point of this passage is that all spiritual gifts have value. So we should never belittle or praise one's gifts. Instead, all Christians have a role in the body of Christ, and all roles are equally important to God.

God also wants Christians to perform certain duties in the body. One of those duties is to confront demonic forces; however, many believers refuse to confront demonic forces. Unfortunately, there is complacency within the church about deliverance, especially in the United States. As a result, most Christians are content with their church routine. So they have no desire to pursue the higher callings-- such as deliverance. Given this, the church is neglecting its responsibility to confront demonic forces in the world.

Most Christians will never confront someone who is demonically possessed; however, they will interact with individuals who are spiritually oppressed at times. Many of these oppressed people will be Christians. Sadly, Christians are oppressed because of unconfessed sins. Likewise, many times these sins are generational. Furthermore, often believers are not aware of generational sins and how they get passed down. As a result, they don't confront the demons associated with generational sins.

As previously noted, family history of alcoholism, drug addiction, pornography, violence, and anger are examples of generational sins. Furthermore, once generational sins have been established within families, they affect all household members. And in time, generational sins become curses. Also, once a curse is established within a bloodline, demonic spirits are attached to it. These bloodline curses are never broken within families because only born-again Christians have the authority to break generational curses. Given this, saved individuals must recognize family curses and confront the demonic spirits attached to them. If they don't, they will continue to be hindered by these oppressive spirits despite their conversion. Unfortunately, most Christians have never been taught anything about curses and why they get attached to families and individuals.

Within the Bible, there are warnings about curses. Most of these warnings pertained to the Israelites and their enemies. Nevertheless, warnings about curses apply to Christians today. For example, we find in Proverbs 26:2 a short but concise verse concerning curses: **Like a flitting sparrow, like a flying swallow, So a curse without cause shall not alight.** Although this is symbolic language, the meaning is clear: demonic spirits need justification to attach curses to individuals or families. They get their justification based on sinful acts that are grievous or obsessive. Furthermore, grievous sins like alcoholism, adultery, or greed are common for nonbelievers. In contrast, sins like unforgiveness, bitterness, or anger are common curses among believers.

Many Christians dismiss the possibility their anger, bitterness, or unforgiveness toward others could be cursed. Instead, they view curses as something God used against the Israelites of the Old Testament due to disobedience. Yet there are verses in the New Testament that imply believers can be inflicted with curses based on what they think or do. For instance, in Ephesians 4:26–27, Christians are given a warning about going to bed angry. **"Be angry, and do not sin" do not let the sun go down on your wrath, nor give place to the devil.** This verse states that negative thoughts have spiritual consequences. Still, the devil cannot read our thoughts but can hear our words and see our actions.

All Christians struggle with sin and temptation daily. These are not physical struggles, but spiritual ones. Therefore, believers need to recognize the snares of the world, flesh, and the devil. Still, there will be days when one's sinful nature wins out; however, this is not proof one is fighting a generational curse. So even though sins of lust, drunkenness, anger, bitterness, or idol worship can be generational curses, it takes more than occasional discretion to confirm the existence of a curse. In contrast, evidence of a generational curse consists of more than an occasional transgression or bad behavior. Instead, it's a spiritual affliction that never goes away without God's intervention.

Signs of Generational Curses

All families deal with physical and emotional issues. Even though some of these issues like mental illness are severe, this does not confirm the existence of a generational curse. Instead, generational curses are persistent, continuous, never-ending afflictions that never get resolved or removed from families. Although things like substance abuse, pornography, violence, bitterness, or unforgiveness can all be learned behaviors, they can also be afflictions that confirm the existence of generational curses. Therefore, the factor that separates learned behavior from a curse is the resiliency of the affliction. Because of this, if you take all the actions necessary to treat an affliction and it remains-- this could be confirmation of a curse.

Even within Christian families, generational curses are common. For Christian men, the spirit of pornography and pride are common. Whereas for Christian women the spirit of offense and bitterness are common. No, not every thought or action based on these conditions is evidence of a family curse. Still, if your grandparents, parents, and you have dealt with the same issue this could be confirmation of a curse.

Generational afflictions within families are not learned behavior because of one's environment. Instead, these afflictions will follow you even after leaving the household. So even if you are active in your church, read your Bible daily, and pray often these activities don't remove curses. To remove a curse, you must ask God for discernment. In short, you must ask God whether a curse is operating within your family. If so, are you willing to do what the Holy Spirit tells you?

Many Christian families are never delivered from generational curses. The reason: We have an adversary. His name is Satan. Given this, once a person is saved, the devil knows he lost his soul. Thereafter, the devil hinders you from bringing others to Christ or growing spiritually. Since he knows the power at your disposal when you ask anything in Jesus's name. One of those things is deliverance from hindering spirits assigned to you based on generational curses.

The word here is *spirits because* demons work as a team. Hence, you may have a spirit of anger, strife, and contention assigned to you. Despite this, you demand in Jesus's name that these spirits be removed from you and against your family. Yet often Christians don't understand or realize that a curse is operating within their family. So they don't connect the spiritual dots. As a result, only after getting married to an outsider will the affliction be brought to light by their spouse. Often wives can see these issues within their husbands. Even non-believing wives can perceive something is off with their husbands.

Christian men, however, often get offended by the notion that something is off. The key, however, for a breakthrough is whether the husband loves his wife. If so, he'll eventually listen to his wife. Nevertheless, due to previous failed relationships or divorces, trust must first be established between the husband and wife before deliverance can be achieved. The reason: The devil will use those past failed relationships to block spiritual discernment.

Although spiritual trials are not popular, sometimes they are necessary for spiritual breakthroughs. In James 1:2–4, we get confirmation of the benefits of trials: **My brethren, count it all joy when you fall into various trials, knowing that the testing of your faith produces patience. But let patience have its perfect work, that you may be perfect and complete, lacking nothing.** These verses are often cited by pastors; however, many believers do not view trials as blessings. Conversely, many believers view difficult situations as attacks from Satan, whereas others think it's just bad luck. Although both views have merit, God uses difficult situations for his purposes--even if he is not responsible for them. Thus, spiritual trials will either increase faith and discernment or embitter one against God.

No doubt spiritual trials can increase faith and reliance on God. Yet sometimes the intervention of others is necessary to reveal afflictions and root causes for them. This can be done in many ways. The first way is to seek out Christian counseling from pastors or strong believers. This is not always easy to do for most Christians, especially men. Since Christian men are taught to be leaders of their homes and providers. So admitting they have problems is a sign of weakness.

A second reason Christians don't seek help from their church is due to wrong doctrines. For instance, many denominations tell their members not to speak the wrong words or the issue will get worse. Hence, they don't admit their problems. Instead, they say all is good. This is a distortion of

Scripture. On the contrary, the Bible says to pray for one another. Yes, there is a place and time when you watch what you say, but if you're under affliction by a generational curse admit the problem.

On a personal note, after retiring from the army, I went through a dark period in my life where anger consumed me. As a result, my marriage ended in divorce. I subsequently attended counseling sessions and took medication for my anger. However, neither approach stopped nor controlled my anger. Finally, I decided to ask for prayer from my church and requested pastoral counseling. Although my pastor did not understand why I was angry, he knew there was a dark spirit in me. In short, a spirit of anger.

At the time, I had no concept of generational curses, nor did I understand anything about oppressive spirits. Despite this, I asked God to take this dark presence off me. To my amazement, I gained control of my anger and realized how Satan used it through the years to hinder me. No, the anger did not dissipate overnight since there were other components to it. There was a physical, emotional, psychological, and spiritual component to my anger. Each area had to be addressed. Although prayer and reliance on God were the keys to my deliverance, I also had to live alone for a while to address the emotional and psychological wounds.

Given my past anger, my family had a wait-and-see attitude towards me. Although I understand now why my family had this attitude towards me, their lack of support prolonged full deliverance. Although I experienced fierce spiritual warfare before my deliverance, the ordeal transformed my relationship with God. Thus, I became aware of God's presence. I became aware of God's presence because of the Holy Spirit.

As a result, God's presence now dictates my daily decisions. Given my spiritual journey, I know Christians must experience a spiritual transformation before God can truly use them. Yes, many believers are faithful and serve God in different ways. Nevertheless, a powerful Christian testimony constitutes death to self. This also extends to believers who want deliverance from generational curses. Since the root causes for generational curses are not physical or emotional, but spiritual. In Mark 8:35, we get confirmation that one must die to self to serve Christ: **For whoever desires to save his life will lose it, but whoever loses his life for My sake and the gospel's will save it.**

The Bible says in this world, we will have trouble. All Christians and nonbelievers would agree with this statement. Despite this, not every physical, mental, or spiritual problem is due to generational curses. Instead, a lot of the bad things we experience are due to a fallen world, a sinful nature, bad decisions, and Satan. Therefore, blaming demons for all your problems won't solve them. In contrast, it will frustrate you and undermine your faith. Given this, learning how to identify generational curses is the key.

The first key to recognizing the presence of a generational curse is to know the signs that one is in effect. Although there are many ways to confirm generational curses, some common signs are as follows:

- A major affliction such as alcoholism, drugs, violence, pornography, anger, bitterness, or unforgiveness has always plagued your family through the years. Furthermore, no counseling or treatment method ever works to remove the affliction. Also, other family members suffer from similar mental and physical ailments.

- There is a negative mindset within the family.

- No one within the extended family will acknowledge the affliction.

- No one within the family overcomes the affliction.

- No one within the family is born- again.

- Despite church activities by family members, prayers don't get answered.

  - Family members are always restless and impatient.

This is a baseline checklist to confirm the existence of a generational curse. Likewise, this checklist can help determine if a difficult situation is based on a curse. If not, ask God for discernment on the matter. Sadly, most Christians only pray when they want something or experience a crisis. Yet God is neither Santa Claus nor Dr. Phil. Instead, God expects you to love him with all your heart, mind, and strength. When you have that type of relationship with the creator of the universe, no good thing will God withhold from you. So, if you're a Christian, and the spiritual evidence confirms a curse, ask God to remove it. This spiritual tenet is confirmed in James 4:7: **Therefore submit to God. Resist the devil**

22

and he will flee from you. Although this verse is short, it's clear and to the point.

For a Christian, resisting refers to your thought patterns because Satan uses them against you. In addition, when oppressive spirits are involved due to generational curses, you're also dealing with a physical presence. Although oppressive spirits can and do torment Christians, they cannot possess them. So even though dark spirits can enter Christians, they cannot remove the Holy Spirit from them. Given this, one must rely on the power of the Holy Spirit to resist any dark presence.

A perfect analogy for how demonic entities enter Christians is like revolving doors—because demons enter in and leave believers quickly. This is not conjecture. I've witnessed this transformation among loved ones and others. Although it's disconcerting and scary, one has the authority to expel these demons from people and themselves. The key is not to be fearful when confronting an oppressive spirit. Remember, the Word says greater is He who is in you than He who is in the world.

Hindering Factors

All born-again Christians have the authority to expel demonic spirits from others and themselves. Yet many believers do not understand this authority. They don't understand this authority because few pastors are willing to address it. They won't address this topic because it's controversial and not uplifting. Instead, pastors prefer sermons their members expect to hear and understand.

Although many pastors recognize the effects of demonic affliction on their members, they don't know how to help them. Yes, many pastors will pray with their members during counseling sessions; however, the core issue behind their affliction is not addressed. In addition, even those pastors who understand what oppressive spirits can do, don't know the hindering factors responsible for one's affliction.

The first factor to recognize is that oppressive spirits are invisible. So even though you feel the effects of demonic attacks physically and emotionally, you cannot see the culprit behind them. In 2 Corinthians 4:18, Paul provides us insight into invisible things: **While we do not look at the things which are seen, but at the things which are not seen. For** the things which are seen are temporary, but the things which are not seen are eternal. The unseen and eternal things could also apply to demonic oppression that prevents individuals from coming to Christ.

Although Satan and his demons are real, many pastors have regulated Satan as an insignificant player in our daily lives. In short, he is out there, but Christ defeated him on the cross. Yes, there is truth to this statement; however, Satan is not an insignificant player. In 1 Peter 5:8, we are told about Satan's purpose: **Be sober, be vigilant; because your adversary the devil walks about like a roaring lion, seeking whom he may devour.** This passage confirms Satan's agenda. That agenda is to stop Christians in any way possible. Yet many of the devices of the devil are invisible. So Christians must keep their spiritual guard up by relying on the Holy Spirit for discernment.

Family

The next hindering factor to consider is our family. Even though families can provide tremendous support during tough times, they can be manipulated by the enemy to prevent spiritual deliverance. This is especially true within Christian households. Chiefly because many Christians believe the devil has no authority to touch or torment them if they go to church and practice their faith.

Although active church involvement can strengthen one against temptation and oppression, believers must still put every thought captive and test every spirit. This is crucial because when one leaves home their faith can be tested. Thereafter, if one falls away from the Lord, how their family treats and supports them can make all the difference. Given this, family members citing Scripture to them to return to the Lord won't work. Instead, what works is intercessory prayer and unconditional love for them.

This is especially true for Christians who do not understand demonic oppression. Yes, Christians can be spiritually oppressed. The only question is whether the oppression is due to a generational curse or hidden sin. As previously noted, most pastors do not understand how to deliver their members from demonic oppression. Likewise, most believers have never been taught about demonic oppression. Yet the key for deliverance for a wayward child is to recognize the spirit behind their oppression.

So when a family member falls away from the Lord, there may be dark forces at work. If so, insisting they go back to church and confess their sins won't work. Also, the oppressed family member may get offended, which allows Satan greater control over them. When this occurs, one must separate their hurt feelings from the facts at hand. So identifying why one fell away from the Lord is crucial. Furthermore, did they engage in some demonic activity that gave the devil a foothold in their life?

Even if one was brought up in a strong Christian home, there were probably relationship issues they experienced through the years. Some of these issues may have been minor offenses, which have always bothered them. Whereas in extreme cases, there may have been physical or sexual abuse in one's household. Whether these offenses are real or perceived, they are viewed differently by one's two natures: their natural and spiritual man. Given this struggle between our two natures, if one is not a mature believer, one's natural man will control how they think on matters. This is important to note because it's the reason why one never gets delivered from their demonic oppression.

A believer's family's opinion of them is another factor to consider. In short, family members know their strengths and weaknesses. Hence, if someone falls away from the Lord, they may blame one's shortfalls. This is a common reaction among nonbelieving households when family members get in trouble. In Christian households, though, judgments are often expressed when children go awry. So whether one's situation occurred because of bad judgment or an oppressive spirit the devil will use this situation to weaken them. Likewise, the devil will use one's family's ridicule to keep them oppressed. Sadly, in extreme cases, this ridicule can force one to abandon their faith.

Even in strong Christian households, relatives tend to underestimate each other spiritually. This can be expected in most households; moreover, we get an illustration of this in the Bible about those who questioned Jesus. In Matthew 13:54–57 the people who knew Jesus best questioned him: **When He had come to His own country, He taught them in their synagogue, so that they were astonished and said, "Where did this Man get this wisdom and these mighty works? Is this not the carpenter's son? Is not His mother called Mary? And**

His brothers James, Joses, Simon, and Judas? And His sisters are they not all with us? Where then did this Man get all these things?" So they were offended at Him. But Jesus said to them, "A prophet is not without honor except in his own country and in his own house." If people felt this way about Jesus, they would question you too. Although it's difficult to accept, you cannot change how family members and others view you. This applies to both Christians and nonbelievers. Furthermore, if you are a born-again Christian, but your family members are not, you'll endure resentment and skepticism about your commitment to Christ.

On a personal note, I experienced this reaction with my family when I accepted Christ after leaving home to join the Army. Thereafter, I endured a lot of criticism from my family about my Christian faith. As a result, it took years before my family accepted my faith as genuine. In addition, I had to learn to love them unconditionally before I stopped judging them. I also discovered years later my family had a generational curse.

No doubt the support from a Christian family can strengthen you during tough times. Despite this, you must recognize your family may not understand spiritual affliction. Therefore, getting upset or judging them is not justified. Given this, if you are under spiritual oppression, the Lord expects you to confront these demons because you have the power to expel them from yourself and others. Likewise, you have the power to change the direction of your bloodline by confessing and demanding that generational curses be removed. In 1 John 4:4 a short verse that confirms this point: **You are of God, little children, and have overcome them, because He who is in you is greater than he who is in the world.**

Pastors and Christians often cite this verse, but they don't apply it. What they don't apply is the power they have in Jesus's name to confront demonic entities. As an example, consider the fear and deterrence a gun has against a would-be intruder. Yet if that gun is unloaded, it's useless. Conversely, if the gun is loaded, it becomes a powerful means of self-defense. Likewise, one must know how to use that gun. If they don't know how to use their gun, it serves no useful purpose. This same rationale applies to the spiritual realm. In short, knowing one has the power in Jesus's name to confront demons.

Deliverance

If all signs indicate a demonic presence, it must be confronted. Although confronting demonic spirits requires a lot of faith and trust in God, you have the authority to expel them. Therefore, to strengthen and encourage you, ask other strong believers to pray with you. Do not be fearful when you pray. Instead, have confidence that God can deliver you from your affliction. The following outline covers the points you need to address when praying for spiritual deliverance:

Lord God in Heaven, I submit myself to you. I ask for your help in this process of deliverance. I know I have authority over all the power of the enemy, according to Luke 10:19, because I truly believe Jesus is your resurrected Son, who died for my sins.

Lord God, I pray you will allow me to repent for my sins of____. Lord, knowingly or unknowingly, I ask that you please break this spirit from my life so that I may fully serve you, Lord. Thank you for your forgiveness, Lord.

Say the next part repeatedly until the manifestations stop.

And now, in the mighty name of my Lord and Savior, Jesus Christ, I declare the spirit of_____ to be broken off my life. I break every single legal right and chain you have over my life, and I proclaim it to be null and void, to fall to the ground and be as dust under my feet in Jesus's mighty name. I plead the blood of Jesus Christ over my heart, mind, body, and soul. I command you, spirit of___, to clean up your filth, pick up your seeds, and leave me now in the name of Jesus Christ.

I repeat, leave *now* in the name of Jesus. I rebuke you. I command you to leave and go immediately into the abyss, and I forbid you from returning to me. I am giving you direct orders in the name of Jesus Christ. Leave now in the name of Jesus. I bind you and loosen you not by my power but by the power of the Holy Spirit, and in the name of Jesus, you are ordered to leave now.

Repeat the prayer until you feel in your spirit the presence has left you. For many reasons, most Christians won't attempt a spiritual deliverance alone. Instead, they prefer their pastor or other strong believers to pray with them for deliverance. There is nothing wrong with this approach. Unlike spiritual possession (total control), oppression is just a hindering force that consumes you at times. Yes, you may feel powerless when the full effect of an oppressive spirit is on you; however, you're not helpless to resist this force—you just feel that way. There is one thing you must remember after a deliverance: it takes time for God to change you. So, you may not feel the full effects of deliverance immediately. Yet those who prayed with you believed you've been delivered. Therefore, you must agree with them. Likewise, expect the devil to immediately test your commitment and faith.

In view of this, if dark thoughts return, you must immediately reject them. How? By proclaiming in Jesus's name that you've been delivered from the curse of____, and you refuse to accept these thoughts.

So, spirit of_____, get out of my head and life. In Jesus's name, I pray.

This spiritual principle is effective and powerful; however, the devil will try to convince you otherwise.

Chapter 2

Satan/Karma

Few would dispute there is evil in the world. The only disagreement is why there is evil in the world. Sociologists contend people are simply a by-product of their culture. So if they do evil acts that are acceptable within their culture, they are not evil. Conversely, they contend that different cultures have no right to judge other ones that practice different values and religious beliefs. In short, no one is right or wrong. They are just a by-product of their culture.

The argument against this premise is that many people reject their cultural values and beliefs. If people reject their cultural norms, then what governs their behavior? If it's based on free will, then why do some people behave responsibly while others are irresponsible? If individuality or free will determines how one acts within a culture, then why would a person choose to reject acceptable behavior when there are negative consequences for doing so? This seems to conflict with the theory that we evolved because of our superior intelligence. Granted, our technology has evolved, but mankind's behavior has not.

Even within cultures where traditional religious beliefs are not taught, people have a sense of what is right and wrong. This moral paradigm can be observed among children with no religious upbringing too. So clearly human beings have been imprinted with something at birth that provides them with a moral compass. Therefore, if we are born with a moral compass or soul, do we concede that God is responsible for it?

If mankind was created with a moral compass or soul, then why do so many people reject the religious tenets of their culture? For example, 70 percent of Americans consider themselves Christians, but many do not attend church often nor do they practice the moral teachings of the faith. Given this, are these individuals Christians? If not, what are the factors that prove one is a Christian?

Most theologians would agree Christians believe that Jesus Christ was the Son of God, who died for their sins. Likewise, because of Jesus, mankind's relationship with God the Father was restored. A relationship that was severed because of Adam's original sin in the garden. Although there are many Christian denominations in the world, the belief that Jesus was the Son of God unites all believers.

Satan

There are two other principles of Christianity that most theologians agree on is that our soul never dies, and we have free will. The Bible seems to imply that angels and demons are immortal too, and they have free will. This is important because it provides an explanation for evil in the world. Since evil is not a feeling, but a negative force that is afflicting mankind. The Bible is clear that the evil force in the world is Satan and his demons.

Satan is called the adversary because he torments mankind and prevents Christians from doing good works. If true, then why did God create a devil? In the Book of Revelation, we are told about Satan's punishment for defying God: **And war broke out in heaven: Michael and his angels fought with the dragon; and the dragon and his angels fought, but they did not prevail, nor was a place found for them in heaven any longer. So the great dragon was cast out, that serpent of old, called the devil and Satan, who deceives the whole world; he was cast to the earth, and his angels were cast out with him.** (Rev. 12:7–9) These verses outline the devil's fate and the consequences for mankind because of it.

As noted in this passage, God did not create a devil, but an archangel named Lucifer. His fall from Heaven was due to his disobedience. Satan's coup in Heaven occurred because he believed his power rivaled that of God's-- even though God created him. No doubt Satan had unique powers and gifts other angels believed in. This was evident because one-third of the angels in Heaven followed him. I think many theologians have underestimated how powerful and gifted Satan was in Heaven.

Satan still has power today, which he uses to attack mankind and cause bad things to happen in the world. His main weapons are demonic persuasion and temptation. Satan uses these weapons to attack our minds with negative thoughts. Despite this, people have free will to reject or accept his evil thoughts. Therefore, for a demonic thought to take hold, a person must agree with it and then act on it. Even the original sin by Adam and Eve was an agreement to do what Satan suggested.

One of the consequences for mankind because of original sin was forfeiting control of the Earth to Satan. We find many verses in the New Testament to support this claim. For example, in the Book of Matthew, there is an interplay between Jesus and the devil. We find this in Matthew 4:8–10: **Again, the devil took Him up on an exceedingly high mountain, and showed Him all the kingdoms of the world and their glory. And he said to Him,"All these things I will give You if You will fall down and worship me." Then Jesus said to him, "Away with you, Satan! For it is written, You shall worship the Lord your God, and Him only you shall serve."** These verses state that Satan rules this world and has the authority to influence the affairs of mankind. Furthermore, it provides us insight into why there is evil in the world.

Many Christians believe Satan was defeated when Jesus Christ died on the cross for our sins. So his authority to attack and torment Christians ended two thousand years ago. The Bible seems to support this position. Still, Christians must live a life that honors God if they want his hedge of protection from the attacks of Satan and his demons. We find in 1 Peter 5:8 confirmation of this: **Be sober, be vigilant; because your adversary the devil walks about like a roaring lion, seeking whom he may devour.** Peter is not talking to nonbelievers. He is talking to Christians. Therefore, Christians must keep their focus on Jesus Christ by living lives that honor God. If not, there are negative spiritual consequences.

Even people of faith struggle with thinking sinful patterns. Feelings of anger, hate, bitterness, lust, envy, pride, unforgiveness, and covetousness can diminish or destroy a Christian's testimony for Christ. Once Christians lose their testimony for Christ due to bad behavior or thinking patterns, they open the door to Satan. Furthermore, God is not obligated to keep his hedge of protection around Christians who won't forgive others and confess their sins. Given this, we must be on guard against the devil's attacks. We are warned about the devil's tactics in John 10:10: **The thief does not come except to steal, and to kill, and to destroy. I have come that they may have life, and that they may have it more abundantly.**

Given this powerful warning concerning Satan, how can anyone fight off these dark thoughts and avoid bad behaviors that will destroy their testimony for Christ? The Bible provides us with an answer in Ephesians 6:10–18: **Finally, my brethren, be strong in the Lord and in the power of His might. Put on the whole armor of God, that you may be able to stand against the wiles of the devil. For we do not wrestle against flesh and blood, but against principalities, against powers, against rulers of the darkness of this age, against spiritual hosts of wickedness in the heavenly places. Therefore take up the whole armor of God, that you may be able to withstand in the evil day, and having done all, to stand. Stand therefore, having girded your waist with truth, having put on the breastplate of righteousness, and having shod your feet with the preparation of the gospel of peace; above all, taking the shield of faith with which you will be able to quench all the fiery darts of the wicked one. And take the helmet of salvation, and the sword of the Spirit, which is the word of God; praying always with all prayer and supplication in the Spirit, being watchful to this end with all perseverance and supplication for all saints.**

These verses outline all the evil forces against Christians and the means to confront them. Yet one must discern the symbolic language used in these verses. For example, putting on the whole armor of God is a metaphor for the three spiritual weapons Christians need to confront Satan and his demons. Those three weapons are the helmet (your thoughts), shield (God's protection), and sword (the Word of God).

The whole armor of God is not difficult to understand; however, applying it to your life is difficult. It's difficult because you must fight your flesh—your human nature, the world, and Satan. The battle to defeat these three impediments is not a physical one, but a battle of your mind. You must determine in your mind that God is the source of your strength, and through faith in him, you can overcome any obstacle. In short, you must have fanatical faith in God to fight off the attacks of Satan and his demons. This can only be achieved by knowing God-- not by knowing about him. You know God by praying and meditating, reading your Bible consistently, and learning to listen to the inner voice of the Holy Spirit.

To keep our focus on God, we must apply the first component of the whole armor of God--the helmet. The helmet is symbolic of controlling what you see and think. Hence, what you watch on television, the music you listen to, and the people you interact with all influence how you think. So if all these activities along with the people you associate with belittle or ignore the things of God, you'll be vulnerable to attacks from the enemy. Given this, you must guard your mind from seeing and hearing things that provide the devil with an opening to oppress you.

To get your mind to think correctly and in a holy way, you must put information into it that points toward God. No, you don't abandon all your friends and family, but you need to change what you watch on television, listen to on the radio, and the people you want to be around. In addition, you must be involved with a church and read your Bible often. These changes are just the first steps. The hard part is allowing the Holy Spirit to take control of your life. This cannot occur until you are willing to change how you think, act, and believe.

Another component of the whole armor of God is the sword. The sword refers to knowing Scripture or your Bible. In practical terms, it's knowing what the Bible says about a given situation. For example, you're feeling tired and defeated about a situation or person. A verse for this situation would be "I can do all things through Christ who strengthens me" (Phil. 4:13). By citing God's Word instead of resorting to the things of the world, you are expressing faith in God. Remember, God is only obligated to intervene for a person if they express faith in him. Still, it takes time and experience to develop faith in Scripture when things go wrong. So the same mentality that one needs to prepare for a marathon applies to faith in Scripture too. In short, you must apply biblical principles to your daily routine.

Even after Christians learn how to apply the whole armor of God, they are not exempt from demonic attacks. We find confirmation of this in 2 Corinthians 12:7: **And lest I should be exalted above measure by the abundance of the revelations, a thorn in the flesh was given to me, a messenger of Satan to buffet me, lest I be exalted above measure.** This is Paul talking to the Corinthians about his suffering for the cause of Christ. Although Paul did nothing worthy of torment by this demon, God allowed it to keep him humbled. Even though Paul was perhaps the greatest Christian who ever lived, he still had to keep his natural man— his sinful nature in check by relying on God. Hence, this tormenting spirit kept Paul grounded and focused on Jesus Christ.

The main point of 2 Corinthians 12:7 is that God allowed Paul to be tormented by this demon. We don't know how Paul was tormented, but it bothered him. This is confirmed in 2 Corinthians 12:8–9: **Concerning this thing I pleaded with the Lord three times that it might depart from me. And He said to me, "My grace is sufficient for you, for My strength is made perfect in weakness."**

Even though no man suffered more than Paul for the cause of Christ, God still refused to cast off this tormenting spirit. Paul knew why: "lest I be exalted above measure." Paul understood that sometimes suffering is necessary to keep us grounded. Many Christians today refuse to believe God sometimes allows suffering for his purposes. The key, though, is to recognize whether God is allowing suffering for some purpose or whether one is under demonic oppression. If one is under demonic oppression, one must address the demon behind it and cast it out.

Church Views

The church today has three views concerning Satan. The first view is that Satan was defeated two thousand years ago. So Christians have nothing to fear from Satan and his demons because he was defeated when Christ died on the cross. The second view is that Satan is a roaring lion ready to pounce on you. Thus, any sinful activity can instantly cause a demonic attack. The last view contends Satan never existed. Instead, he was created during the Dark Ages to keep people fearful and loyal to the church. Many nonbelievers share this view today. Sadly, many Christians doubt the existence of a literal devil too.

If the devil is not real, then why did Jesus Christ die on the cross for our sins? The answer was to restore our relationship with God the Father because of the original sin of Adam and Eve. Satan caused mankind's separation from God when he deceived Eve into eating the forbidden fruit in the garden. Given this, one cannot claim to be a

Christian and doubt the existence of Satan. One cannot doubt the existence of Satan because since the fall mankind has been thrown into a spiritual war of good versus evil. This is a war for the souls of mankind.

Many Christians do not understand this war. As a result, Satan and his demons are ruling the earth with an iron fist. Given this, the spiritual condition of the world won't change until Christians exercise their authority over Satan by invoking the name of Jesus. So given this spiritual war between the forces of good and evil, pastors must preach about this subject to their congregations. Yet many pastors won't preach about the devil and demonic things.

There are three reasons pastors are reluctant to preach about the devil: First, pastors are scared to lose their ministries because this message is not popular or uplifting. Second, many churches today have lukewarm Christians that lack faith in Christ, and the authority of Scripture. So they cannot accept or discern deep spiritual issues. The third reason is outlined in 2 Corinthians 11:13–15. These verses warn about false teachers: **For such are false apostles, deceitful workers, transforming themselves into apostles of Christ. And no wonder! For Satan himself transforms himself into an angel of light. Therefore it is no great thing if his ministers also transform themselves into ministers of righteousness, whose end will be according to their works.**

Most Christian churches today are pastored by men and women who believe Jesus Christ is the Son of God. So the warning in 2 Corinthians 11:13–15 applies to most pastors today. Still, some Christian ministers today are misleading their congregations with false doctrines. Yet the main culprit for the spiritual decline in the United States is our culture. Mainly because Christians won't reject the secular messages of our culture. Thus, this has weakened the church. As a result, Satan has the church in disarray and is causing havoc throughout the world.

The Satan Effect

There are many factors responsible for why bad things happen to good people. The main reason is Satan and his demons. Yes, Satan is a powerful factor that can be blamed for many of the bad things in the world.

Likewise, there are different aspects or factors associated with Satan. The first Satan factor is God does not protect nonbelievers. Our opinion of who is considered good does not matter to God. Only one who is born-again is justified before God. In Matthew 19:17, Jesus confirms that no one is good except for God: **So He said to him, "Why do you call Me good? No one is good but One, that is, God. But if you want to enter into life, keep the commandments."** One aspect of obeying God's commandments is to accept Jesus as Savior.

Although a Christian's spirit is born again, their soul is not. The soul is our thoughts, emotions, and will. Thus, all Christians must be vigilant to keep their soul and spirit lined up. This cannot be done through human efforts. Instead, it must be done by submitting to the urges of the Holy Spirit that resides in every Christian's heart. So when Christians ignore or refuse to listen to the Holy Spirit, they start a process of disengagement with God. Thereafter, when they engage in sinful activities, they lose their testimony for Christ, which triggers spiritual consequences. Although a single sinful act may not trigger these spiritual consequences, a refusal to repent from it will.

Christians can engage in sinful activities that will break their fellowship with God. As a result, they open themselves up to demonic attacks. For example, excessive drinking or drug use will destroy a Christian's testimony for Christ; moreover, they could lose their life because of it. Likewise, hidden sins such as pornography, gambling, unforgiveness, and bitterness will demoralize Christians, and they will lose their faith in God too. These hidden sins can also generate feelings of hopelessness and doubts about one's salvation. Unfortunately, some Christians even succumb to suicide because of their despair.

When Christians fall out of fellowship with God, they are vulnerable to attacks from Satan. Although Satan cannot read your mind, he can discern patterns of behavior that provide him opportunities to attack you. We get warnings of this in 1 Peter 5:8: **be sober, be vigilant; because your adversary the devil, as a roaring lion, walketh about, seeking whom he may devour.** No, Satan is not everywhere, but he has many demons. These demons have areas of responsibility and individuals to watch over. So Christians need to keep alert for the snares of the enemy.

A Christian's spirit is born again, but their soul is not. The soul wars against the inner voice of the Holy Spirit. So if an unconfessed sin becomes ingrained in a Christian's soul, Satan gains control. Once Satan has control, bad things can happen. Although God is love, he cannot allow Christians to sin with impunity. Given this, God's hedge of protection from Satan can be lifted from Christians when they fail to repent of known sins.

Many Christians and nonbelievers know negative results can occur when people do bad things, yet often they want to blame someone for it. As a result, when loved ones or friends suffer because of bad choices, Christians may cite Satan as the culprit. Still, sometimes faithful Christians will experience periods of suffering. For instance, the tragic loss of a child or spouse without warning can shake even the strongest person of faith. Also, a terminal medical diagnosis of self can invoke fear and anger that God cannot be trusted.

Although Christians know Satan is responsible for many of the bad things that happen in the world directly or indirectly—indirectly due to original sin, it's still hard to accept that bad things happen to us. Also, it's hard for believers to understand why God allows Satan to attack his children for no apparent reason. Although it's frustrating, like Job of the Old Testament, sometimes Christians suffer for unknown reasons.

Karma

Another Satan factor is Karma. Ironically, many Christians have more belief in Karma than a literal devil. What is Karma? We find in Ephesians 6:12 the answer: For we do not wrestle against flesh and blood, but against principalities, against powers, against rulers of the darkness of this age, against spiritual hosts of wickedness in the heavenly places. This passage outlines the dark forces that are formidable and hard to defeat. Paul does not explain how these evil forces attack or hinder us. What he does tell us is to put on the whole armor of God to resist them.

We can, therefore, conclude that *Karma* is a code word for demonic forces controlled by Satan. The words *principalities, powers, rulers of this age,* and *spiritual hosts of wickedness* in Ephesians 6:12 are referring to an evil force controlled by Satan. Each level of this evil force has specific areas of responsibility. This force is an army of demons with the authority to harm the body, mind, and spirit. Within this evil force, there are ranks and powers assigned to demons. The strongest demons are those that rule over nations. These demonic spirits affect all nations. They are assigned to countries based on past sins of the land. For example, the United States' past sin is slavery. Given this, there is a spirit of racial unrest that permeates the country today.

We find biblical evidence of why nations are cursed in the Book of Deuteronomy. God tells the Israelites the awards if they're obedient. Conversely, the Israelites are told the negative consequences if they are disobedient. The blessings are listed in Deuteronomy 28:1–3: **"Now it shall come to pass, if you diligently obey the voice of the Lord your God, to observe carefully all His commandments which I command you today, that the Lord your God will set you high above all nations of the earth. And all these blessings shall come upon you and overtake you, because you obey the voice of the Lord your God: "Blessed shall you be in the city, and blessed shall you be in the country."**

In contrast, God's warning for a nation that is disobedient is listed in Deuteronomy 28:15–16: **"But it shall come to pass, if you do not obey the voice of the Lord your God, to observe carefully all His commandments and His statutes which I command you today, that all these curses will come upon you and over take you: "Cursed shall you be in the city, and cursed shall you be in the country."**

These verses were not just for the nation of Israel, but for all countries. God has put in place spiritual consequences for nations that reject him and his commandments. One factor of these spiritual consequences is demonic oppression for a nation that rejects him and subsequently crosses a spiritual line. For example, the United States has always been considered a Christian country, but those core biblical principles are now under attack. Also, many Christians have compromised their beliefs because of their culture. As a result, the country is experiencing tremendous spiritual and social unrest. Given this, Christians must be faithful and intercede for the country.

Tongue

Another aspect of Karma is the power of our tongues or words to cause harm. A common adage I was told as a child "Sticks and stones can break my bones, but words can never hurt me" is perhaps the greatest lie children are told. Harsh words do affect children and adults. For example, most marriages end because of communication problems. These communication problems developed over time due to heated arguments, which destroyed trust and created resentment within the marriage.

Many marital arguments occur because of misspoken words. Even when there are real issues within a marriage that can be resolved, how the parties speak to each other can make the difference. Unfortunately, men do not understand how their words affect women. Whereas women do not understand that men yell without thinking about the consequences of their words. If men and women would recognize how the other sex speaks and processes words, they would not get offended and hurt so quickly. Thus, relationships and marriages could be saved.

Most people would agree it's difficult not to gossip, express their opinions, or respond when someone is criticizing them. Although we know there are consequences for speaking our minds, we still do it. In the Book of James, we are told about the tongue. We find this in James 3:8: **But no man can tame the tongue. It is an unruly evil, full of deadly poison.** If this were the only verse in the Bible that spoke about the tongue, we could consider it a metaphor; however, there are many biblical verses concerning the tongue and how it affects us. For example, in James 3:5–6, we get a detailed description of the wrongs of the tongue: **Even so the tongue is a little member and boasts great things. See how great a forest a little fire kindles! And the tongue is a fire, a world of iniquity. The tongue is so set among our members that it defiles the whole body, and sets on fire the course of nature; and it is set fire by hell.**

The power of words to motivate or discourage is clear. Great coaches and politicians have learned that words can motivate people to do things. Conversely, harsh words can demoralize individuals, especially children. God's original intent was for mankind to use his tongue for good things; however, the fall changed that purpose. Given this, Satan knows the power we have in our tongues if we speak the wrong things.

Karma Keys

Karma does exist, but it's not some mysterious force that affects only people who do wrong. Instead, Karma is a combination of demonic factors that are triggered by acts of individuals or nations. Many of these spiritual factors are passed down from one generation to another. Likewise, the sins of nations or regions are affixed and cannot be removed until God's people intercede on behalf of the land.

Christians must also realize that family generational curses and judgments are another aspect of Karma. For example, family generational sins such as alcoholism, drug use, pornography, or suicide will continue to be passed down until a born-again Christian breaks the curse. Furthermore, only spirit-filled Christians within the bloodline can break family curses and judgments.

Karma is also triggered by the words we speak. The Bible is clear that our words have the power to do good or evil. In Proverbs 15:1–4, we are told about the power of the tongue to do good or evil: **A soft answer turns away wrath, But a harsh word stirs up anger. The tongue of the wise uses knowledge rightly, But the mouth of fools pours forth foolishness. The eyes of the Lord are in every place, Keeping watch on the evil and the good. A wholesome tongue is a tree of life, But perverseness in it breaks the spirit**. These verses confirm that how we use our words can affect people either positively or negatively. We also find in Proverbs 18:21 a dire warning of what an evil tongue can do: **Death and life are in the power of the tongue, And those who love it will eat its fruit.**

Although pastors boldly proclaim the defeat of Satan when Jesus Christ died on the cross, they won't preach about the aspects of Karma we trigger by our actions in words and deeds. Mainly because these spiritual principles require a greater understanding of the war between God and evil. A war that cannot be won unless Christians understand the authority they have in Jesus's name to confront the devil's devices. Conversely, if Christians don't exercise the authority they have in Jesus to confront demonic forces, they will be suppressed and oppressed until they embrace the full armor of God.

Chapter 3

Physical Signs

The devil knows the power Christians have in Jesus's name to change situations. Given this, he plans his attacks against us based on our spiritual strengths and weaknesses. So even though we are unique individuals with spiritual gifts from God, oppressive spirits can hinder us based on many factors. One factor is the church we attend. Although the church we attend may not be a negative factor, what they don't teach could be. For instance, the Catholic church and traditional Protestant denominations do not instruct their members about spiritual warfare. As a result, many Christians who attend these churches cannot discern a random chance event from a spiritual attack by the devil.

The devil and his demons are invisible to the naked eye. So many Christians cannot recognize when they are under demonic attacks. The devil wants to keep it that way. Although mature believers may suspect demonic activity when something bad happens to them or others, they may have doubts about it. Given this, often Christians won't address oppressive spirits when praying about the matter. Instead, they will pray about the situation. Although God may answer their prayers, they may be delayed or not answered because the core issue is not addressed. Conversely, if believers would pray about the oppressive spirits inflicting them, one's deliverance from these demonic attacks could occur immediately.

Many Christians become frustrated and disappointed with God when their prayers are not answered, yet they ignore possible spiritual factors that are hindering their prayers. Two spiritual factors are unconfessed sins and generational curses. Many Christians do not understand how the devil uses these sins and curses to oppress them. Despite this, sometimes God will intervene and reveal these hindering spirits to you. God does this through revelations, dreams, or prophetic words from other believers. In addition, sometimes God allows demonic physical manifestations to open your eyes.

Physical Things

The thought of seeing demons or feeling their presence terrifies many Christians. Therefore, God won't expose demonic spirits to you unless he has a purpose for it, and you have the spiritual maturity to handle it. Further, this type of spiritual maturity can only occur once you have an intimate relationship with Jesus Christ. This is necessary because nothing else can prepare you for the intense fear of seeing or feeling demonic spirits.

There is a popular show on cable television called *GhostAdventures*. This program depicts a team of psychic researchers that investigate the existence of trapped spirits at haunted locations. The show narrator often implies the dark spirits they encounter are deceased people, and they are trapped there due to some misfortune. Conversely, the narrator is reluctant to call dark spirits demons. Instead, he will often suggest there is a negative energy at these sites. As a result, this research team always concludes there is something supernatural in these haunted locations, but they cannot identify or remove it.

This psychic research team routinely interviews people who have had encounters with demonic spirits. Furthermore, many of these individuals blamed Satan and his demons for their torment. Despite this, the narrator is reluctant to cite Satan as the culprit behind their oppression. This position is puzzling considering this team filmed a Christian deliverance. This Christian deliverance episode filmed by the research team covered one session of a priest praying for a man. The oppressed man in this session felt a dark presence come over him during the deliverance, but it left him. Then once the session was over the man is shown hugging his loved ones. Thereafter, the show narrator implies the man was delivered. Despite this, the narrator won't acknowledge that the devil was responsible for this man's oppression.

In many ways, the narrator in *Ghost Adventures* won't openly acknowledge the possibility there is evil in the world because of Satan. Instead, he implies dark spirits are tormented souls that cannot move on, yet he provides no proof to support his premise. Conversely, the Bible is clear when a person dies their spirit leaves the body and is transported to a different realm. In Ecclesiastes 3:20–21, Solomon clearly explains the disposition of our bodies and spirits when we die: **All go to one place: all are from the dust, and all return to dust. Who knows the spirit of the sons of men, which goes upward, and the spirit of the animal, which goes down to the earth?** There is no symbolic or figurative language in these verses; therefore, the literal interpretation applies.

Even though the narrator of *Ghost Adventures* advocates a misleading belief about dark spirits, the program does show many of the physical ailments caused by oppressive spirits. For instance, many times members of the *Ghost Adventures* research team will experience episodes of fear, anxiety, or disorientation while exploring these haunted sites. Sometimes, these feelings are so overwhelming the members of the team flee the area. These types of occurrences are proof oppressive spirits are at these locations-- even though the reasons for these demonic attacks are not known. Still, these haunted sites are cursed. The only question is whether an individual or a group caused the curse.

I only watch *Ghost Adventures* occasionally because I know this psychic research team is documenting demonic spirits at work. Although many nonbelievers find this show entertaining, they don't realize what they're watching. Sadly, the physical afflictions revealed in this program can happen to anyone-- especially nonbelievers. And unlike the show, attacks by oppressive spirits do not go away after an hour. Instead, once an individual becomes a target of oppressive spirits there is no relief from it until a Christian deliverance is conducted. This is necessary because only the authority we have in Jesus's name can deliver people from demonic spirits.

On a personal note, I have experienced many of the afflictions shown in *Ghost Adventures*. In addition, I have heard personal testimonies from family members, friends, and other people concerning their experiences with demonic spirits. Likewise, many of these accounts were similar. For instance, a common attack by oppressive spirits involves intense fear and anxiety. This is not a normal fear or anxiety, but an overwhelming feeling that consumes them at times. Further, sometimes these intense feelings only surface at certain locations or around certain people. When these feelings occur around certain people or sites, one is dealing with oppressive spirits.

People do experience bouts of anxiety and fear that are not due to demonic attacks. In addition, many people have cognitive issues because of physical or psychological trauma. Nevertheless, if you suspect that something unusual is causing your fear or anxiety, ask God for discernment. Remember, the Word says to ask, knock, and seek. So if you are a born-again Christian, God must answer your prayer. Given this, a spiritual point to remember about overwhelming fear and anxiety: an event triggered it, even if the event was not spiritual.

Intense fear, anxiety, or disorientation could also be your reactions to things that unnerve you. For example, I hate snakes, and when I see one, I experience fear and anxiety. Still, my initial fearful feelings fade once I view the situation logically. So, I don't stay frozen by fear and anxiety that can consume me. Conversely, when one experiences a sudden attack of fear or anxiety for no apparent reason this is not natural. Instead, this could be confirmation of a demonic attack. Furthermore, the devil will disguise his attacks against you. As a result, you don't exercise your authority in Jesus's name to stop them. So one needs to understand that Satan knows your spiritual strengths and weaknesses, and he will use them against you.

The last possibility for uncontrolled fear and anxiety is cursed items in your home. These items could be anything, even simple tourist trinkets from a foreign country; however, the item is not the issue. Instead, the issue is whether something demonic is associated with it. Furthermore, one's belief or disbelief in demonic attachments does not mitigate the effects of cursed items. The key is to recognize when something changes in one's home, and whether this change occurred after bringing in some item.

In summation, intense feelings of fear, anxiety, and disorientation can be physical signs of oppressive spirits. The only question is why? If the oppression is due to generational curses or personal sins, then you cite the deliverance prayer in chapter 1. Conversely, if these attacks only occur around certain people or at certain locations, you avoid these individuals and places. Furthermore, you ask God for discernment concerning these individuals and places.

Cursed Items

Many people do not realize that cursed items can affect them. Even Christians can be affected by cursed items. Yet because of Hollywood movies, many people believe cursed items are associated with mummies or evil people of the past. Instead, cursed items could be anything associated with witchcraft, idolatry, Satan worship, or voodoo. Although most Christians would never bring anything into their home that was cursed, they may not realize an item they received or purchased was cursed.

In Deuteronomy 7, God outlines the benefits to the Israelites if they're obedient. Conversely, God tells the Israelites in Deuteronomy 7:26 the dire consequences of cursed items: **Nor shall you bring an abomination into your house, lest you be doomed to destruction like it. You shall utterly detest it and utterly abhor it, for it is an accursed thing.** Although this verse is referring to carved images of pagan gods, this could be anything that might be an idol. An idol could be anything you value or place more faith in than God.

After *The Exorcist* was released, people were leery about purchasing Ouija boards. But that is no longer the case today. Instead, the Ouija board, tarot cards, and crystal balls have now become popular. Sadly, people do not realize that dabbing with things of the occult opens the door to demonic attacks. So Christians should never bring into their homes known demonic items such as Ouija boards, tarot cards, or crystal balls.

Another warning for Christians about cursed items involve visiting countries with histories of demonic activity. Many items sold to tourists in these countries could be cursed. For example, when you visit places like New Orleans or the Caribbean Islands, these places have a history of voodoo. Although voodoo is not a common practice in these areas today, the spirit behind it remains in these areas. Furthermore, there are still individuals practicing voodoo in these places. Given this, you must always be leery of purchasing any items that may be associated with voodoo practices. So as a Christian, when you visit places that have a history of Satanic practices, you must use discretion before buying a souvenir. You need to use discretion because there may be something dark associated with the souvenirs.

The monetary value of an item does not matter. What matters is what the souvenir represents. For example, cute little voodoo dolls are items you should never buy. Since these items are tools used in voodoo spells and ceremonies. Likewise, unless you know the history of a souvenir in a country--don't buy it. This is especially true for non-Christian countries like India. In India, they believe in over three hundred million Gods. Although this figure seems irrational, many Hindus in India embrace God as many. Thus, most souvenirs in India are worship idols that should not be purchased.

Many times Christians will receive or purchase items that are cursed. And unlike what you see in the movies, weird things don't always happen in one's home immediately. Furthermore, if you have not received the baptism of the Holy Spirit, you won't be able to discern whether an item is cursed. Yet you will experience the effects of cursed items. One of these effects involves uneasy feelings, which seem to hinder you from overcoming a problem or sickness. In short, you know something is off, but you cannot figure it out. Given this, you must identify when you first felt this uneasiness. Thereafter, determine if something was brought into your home at that time.

The key point about cursed items is discernment (the ability to choose between what is true and right and what is false and wrong). Given this, it's important to listen to what the Holy Spirit is revealing to you about a situation. Although most Christians will never knowingly bring cursed items into their home, there are still many ways Satan deceives people with items. For example, watching horror movies at home, playing violent video games, or reading suggestive books can all affect your spiritual health. Although these items may not be cursed, how they affect your thinking patterns could be openings for oppressive spirits.

There is a spiritual golden rule all Christians should obey: remove the accursed items from your home. A cursed item could be anything the enemy uses to break you down spiritually. So in addition to dark movies, books, and video games, you must also realize that technology is a double-edged sword. Although the internet and smartphones have improved our lives immensely, they can also be used by Satan to ensnare us with sinful desires. Granted, technology is here to stay, yet you must exercise vigilance and discernment about how the devil can use your devices against you.

Angels and Demons

There are many accounts of angels appearing to people and performing supernatural acts throughout the Bible. Many times, the first reaction these biblical characters felt after seeing an angel was fear. This is not the type of response people expect from an angel encounter. Instead, many people believe angels exist to watch over them. Although there is proof throughout Scripture that angels help people, that is not their primary mission. Their primary mission is to do God's will. Often God's will entails delivering messages. Angels can deliver messages through dreams, visions, or physical manifestations.

Scripture is clear that angels perform many duties. Furthermore, not all angels have the same responsibilities; moreover, some angels are archangels such as Michael and Gabriel. These two angels have tremendous power, but for different purposes, though. For example, Gabriel is God's messenger, and throughout the Bible, he is sent to proclaim miraculous events. Conversely, Michael is a warring angel, and he is sent to enforce God's will against Satan and mankind.

Many Christians can identify with the mission of Gabriel, but not with the duties of Michael. Despite this disconnect, throughout the Bible Michael was sent to kill people and destroy cities. Although many believers find the actions of Michael disturbing, God still uses angels today to carry out his judgments. The strongest evidence of this is the Book of Revelation. So in the last days, angels will carry out many judgments against mankind.

One of the best-known passages in the Bible concerning an angel is listed in Matthew 1:20–21: **But while he thought about these things, behold, an angel of the Lord appeared to him in a dream, saying, "Joseph, son of David, do not be afraid to take to you Mary your wife, for that which is conceived in her is of the Holy Spirit. And she will bring forth a Son, and you shall call His name Jesus, for He will save His people from their sins."** Because of this story, many Christians believe angels only bring good news, yet they don't contemplate the reason why an angel of the Lord delivered this message to Joseph.

In Matthew 1:19, we are told about Joseph's mindset before receiving this revelation from the angel of the Lord: **Then Joseph, her husband, being a just man, and not wanting to make her a public example, was minded to put her away secretly.** The reason Joseph wanted to put Mary away was because she was pregnant, and he was not the father. Although I believe Joseph loved Mary, based on Jewish law, she committed a great sin by getting pregnant. Given Mary's condition, Joseph needed a powerful revelation from God to change his mind about putting her away.

Another point Christians don't contemplate about this message from the angel of the Lord is that without an earthly father, no one would have accepted Jesus as the Son of God. Because during biblical times, who your father was determined how people viewed you. Also, Joseph was a descendant of King David of the Old Testament. This was important because Jesus's lineage had to be traced to King David. This was necessary because biblical prophecy predicted the Messiah would be called the Son of David.

In many ways, the angel account in Matthew 1:20–21 is a revelation encounter. Angels can also reveal messages by appearing to believers. In these encounters, a person will interact with a real angel. Although scoffers may doubt angels exist, much less appear to people, the Bible records several accounts of physical manifestations of angels. For example, one of the earliest angel encounters is recorded in Genesis 19:15–17: **When the morning dawned, the angels urged Lot to hurry, saying, "Arise, take your wife and your two daughters who are here, lest you be consumed in the punishment of the city." And while he lingered, the men took hold of his hand, his wife's hand, and the hands of his two daughters, the Lord being merciful to him, and they brought him out and set him outside the city. So it came to pass, when they had brought them outside, that he said, "Escape for your life! Do not look behind you nor stay anywhere in the plain. Escape to the mountains, lest you be destroyed."**

In Genesis 19:1–14, we are told why angels are in Lot's house and their purpose for being in Sodom. Given this, there are some spiritual points to contemplate in these first fourteen verses of chapter 19. For instance, the angels Lot met at the gate of Sodom looked like men. Lot worshiped them as servants of God, but he did not realize they were angels. Further, Lot was concerned for their safety. As a result, he insisted these angels stay at his house for protection. Also, Lot fed them.

The second point to contemplate is how Lot was protected from the men of Sodom, who wanted to have sex with these two angels. Lot thought he was protecting these angels from the men of Sodom-- even if it meant sacrificing his daughters to protect them. So again, Lot did not realize these men were angels, and they did not need his protection. So only after these angels struck the men of Sodom with blindness did Lot realize they were protecting him. Thereafter, when they told Lot they would destroy the city, he believed them and tried to convince his sons-in-law to flee with him.

Like Lot, people today are experiencing physical encounters with angels, but they don't realize it. There is evidence in Scripture to support this contention. For example, in Hebrews 13:1–2, we get proof angels interact with us as people: **Let brotherly love continue. Do not forget to entertain strangers, for by so doing some have unwittingly entertained angels.** Given this passage and Lot's story, we can conclude that angels can materialize as men. Likewise, they don't reveal themselves as angels. Despite this, I believe anyone who has experienced a physical encounter with an angel will recognize it in time.

Even though most biblical accounts of angel encounters are recorded in the Old Testament, nothing written in the New Testament changed their purposes. What changed after Jesus's death on the cross was the gift of the Holy Spirit, which is given to every true believer in Jesus Christ. Therefore, Christians have the indwelling of the Holy Spirit to guide them daily. Also, they have the authority to access God the Father. In contrast, few Old Testament people had access to God the Father or the indwelling of the Holy Spirit. This is one reason why angels manifested themselves more often in the Old Testament than in the New Testament. Despite this, God still sends angels today to warn, protect, and reveal matters to us.

Satan's Angels

Like God, Satan has an army of angels too; however, their appearance and authority changed after their banishment from Heaven. Thus, demons do not have the same power as angels, but they can still inflict us with physical and mental conditions. Furthermore, unlike angels, demons are meant to hinder not help us. To what extent they hinder us depends on our faithfulness and obedience to the Word. Even strong believers will face opposition from demonic forces, but they have the authority in Jesus's name to confront them.

Most of the attacks of Satan and his demons are against our minds. Satan does this by suggesting bad thoughts to us and then observing our responses to them. If we don't reject his thoughts immediately, he keeps probing until we accept or reject his temptations. So Christians must always remember temptation is not a sin but acting on it would be. Also, God will not allow Satan to attack us beyond our ability to resist him—unless we engage in overt sin.

If God restricts how Satan can attack us, can we assume demons cannot appear as men? There is a passage in the Old Testament that seems to confirm demons once walked on the earth as men. In Genesis 6:1–2, we are told about the Sons of God taking human wives: **Now it came to pass, when men began to multiply on the face of the earth, and daughters were born to them, that the sons of God saw the daughters of men, that they were beautiful; and they took wives for themselves of all whom they chose.** No doubt these sons of God were not men. Some contend they were angels, but others say demons. Scripture seems to suggest they were demons because God soon thereafter destroyed the world due to its wickedness.

Given the spiritual state of the world today, demons do not need to appear as men because the world is oblivious to the war between good and evil. Fortunately for us, this war is being fought in the spiritual realm. So at the end of time, God and his children will prevail. Right now, though, Christians must have faith and do their part to resist the schemes of the enemy. Given this, God won't allow demons to deceive the godly if they are obedient to the Word. So even though the ungodly are controlled and manipulated by demons, Christians are not if they keep their focus on Jesus Christ.

Dark Shadows

Even though Christians have the power to resist the devil, no one wants to see demons because they are hideous and can traumatize us. Despite this, sometimes God allows demons to reveal themselves to us in different ways. These ways could be in dreams, visions, or physical manifestations. Many times, the first born-again Christian within a family will receive spiritual revelations, which may include encounters with demons. Likewise, God gives some Christians the gift of discerning spirits. In short, these individuals can sense demonic bondage within people.

We get biblical confirmation of this gift in 1 Corinthians 12:8–10: **For to one is given the word of wisdom through the Spirit, to another the word of knowledge through the same Spirit, to another faith by the same Spirit, to another gifts of healings by the same Spirit, to another the working of miracles, to another prophecy, to another discerning of spirits, to an other different kinds of tongues, to another the interpretation of tongues.** This passage confirms discerning of spirits is a gift of the Holy Spirit.

I don't have the gift of discerning spirits, but I have family members that do. They often tell me similar stories. A story I often hear about oppressed individuals is that demons know who has the gift of discerning spirits. So they discourage oppressed individuals from seeking their help-- even if the oppressed person wants to be delivered. This occurs because unsaved individuals cannot overrule the dark forces controlling them. In contrast, oppressed Christians can resist demonic forces when they seek out God for deliverance.

Another account I often hear concerns the appearance of dark shadows. These dark shadow appearances occur in places where demonic activity is suspected. Likewise, these shadows are seen around spiritually oppressed individuals. Even Christians can experience sightings of these dark shadows. When these appearances do occur, they are brief. In most cases, the only thing you see is a black shadow moving quickly. You won't see any demons hovering. Instead, most of these occurrences will appear like flashes of darkness darting through a room. These dark shadows are not energy sources or trapped souls. They are demons.

For many years, I wondered about these dark shadows and what they meant. I did not question the honesty of my family members, but I assumed only Christians gifted with discerning spirits could see dark shadows. Yet I had no doubt these dark shadows were demons. So I believed demons wanted to stay hidden from Christians. All this changed after I experienced an encounter with a dark shadow while hospitalized. And like the accounts I heard from family members, a dark shadow raced across my room at high speed. Although it left the room quickly, I knew this dark entity was responsible for my medical condition. Thereafter, after a few more days in the hospital, when the doctors could not find anything wrong with me, I was released. This ended a six-month medical ordeal, which landed me in the hospital three times.

I saw confirmation of my dark shadow experience months later while watching *Ghost Adventures*. In this episode of *Ghost Adventures*, after the research team had set up their recording equipment, they waited until nightfall to probe the building. That evening, as the narrator and coworker probe the building a dark shadow raced across the room. This image is caught on camera; however, no one in the room saw it. Yet the individuals in the room felt something eerie. This dark shadow image is what I saw in my hospital room. Thus, this confirmed what I saw was real and not my imagination.

Although dark shadows are physical manifestations of demons, most Christians will never see them. There are two reasons for this: First, the fear of seeing one would unnerve many believers, especially new Christians. Whereas mature Christians would know these dark shadows are demons. As a result, they would invoke the name of Jesus to expel them. If not, they would seek out Christians who understood spiritual warfare. The enemy knows this too. Given this, Christians need to know Satan and his demons do not fear you. What they fear is the authority you have in Jesus's name to confront them.

Some would argue that dark shadows are not in the Bible, yet throughout the New Testament, Jesus constantly talked about and delivered people from demonic affliction. Take for example Matthew 8:16–17: **When evening had come, they brought to Him many who were demon-possessed. And He cast out the spirits with a word, and healed all who were sick, that it might be fulfilled which was spoken by Isaiah the prophet, saying: "He Himself took out**

infirmities And bore our sicknesses."

This is just one of several accounts throughout the New Testament concerning Jesus casting out demons. Likewise, there are many New Testament accounts of how demons afflicted people. So even though Christians may find the subject of demons disturbing, Jesus had no such reservations about acknowledging and confronting them.

Animals Know

Another physical sign for detecting demons can be observed in animals. The reason for this is because animals seem to have a sixth sense, which human beings do not. As a result, they can detect things we cannot see. For example, animals can sense when natural occurrences are forming. So animals know when tornados, hurricanes, or earthquakes are imminent. Scientists believe animals can detect storms and earthquakes because of their superior senses. Scientists accept this theory because it's rational. Whereas conceding animals have a spiritual sixth sense humans lack is not rational. Despite this, there is evidence in the Bible that animals can detect supernatural things that humans cannot. This includes the ability to detect demons and angels.

Most of the passages in the Bible about animals describe how to sacrifice or eat them. Still, there are verses about animals that imply they have spiritual awareness. This does not mean animals have souls, just an awareness of spiritual things. For example, in Ecclesiastes 3:21, Solomon speaks about the spirits of men and animals and where they go after they die: **Who knows the spirit of the sons of men, which goes upward, and the spirit of the animal, which goes down to the earth?**

The reference to the spirit in this passage does not refer to souls. Instead, it refers to the life source within all living creatures. Thus, the source that gives us life. Given this, animals get their life source from the earth, and human beings are given life by God. Mankind is given life by God because they have souls that never die. Yet even though animals may not have souls, they can detect the presence of angels and demons.

The strongest evidence in the Bible about animals' abilities to sense the supernatural can be found in the Book of Numbers. The backdrop for this story is a servant of God named Balaam, and Balak, the king of the

Moabites. Balak wanted Balaam to curse a people in his land, but God said no. Despite this, Balaam decides to travel with the princes of Moab anyway. As a result, God is angry with Balaam, and he sends the angel of the Lord to stop him. In Numbers 22:22–32, we are told about the angel of the Lord and how he keeps Balaam's donkey off the road: **Then God's anger was aroused because he went, and the Angel of the Lord took His stand in the way as an adversary against him. And he was riding on his donkey, and his two servants were with him. Now the donkey saw the Angel of the Lord standing in the way with His drawn sword in His hand, and the donkey turned aside out of the way and went into the field. So Balaam struck the donkey to turn her back onto the road. Then the Angel of the Lord stood in a narrow path between the vineyards, with a wall on this side and a wall on that side. And when the donkey saw the Angel of the Lord, she pushed herself against the wall and crushed Balaam's foot against the wall; so he struck her again. Then the Angel of the Lord went further, and stood in a narrow place where there was no way to turn either to the right hand or to the left. And when the donkey saw the Angel of the Lord, she lay down under Balaam; so Balaam's anger was aroused, and he struck the donkey with his staff. Then the Lord opened the mouth of the donkey, and she said to Balaam, "What have I done to you, that you have struck me these three times?" And Balaam said to the donkey, "Because you have abused me. I wish there were a sword in my hand, for now I would kill you!" So the donkey said to Balaam, "Am I not your donkey on which you have ridden, ever since I became yours, to this day? Was I ever disposed to do this to you?" And he said, "No." Then the Lord opened Balaam's eyes, and he saw the Angel of the Lord standing in the way with his drawn sword in His hand; and he bowed his head and fell flat in his face. And the Angel of the Lord said to him, "Why have you struck your donkey these three times? Behold, I have come out to stand against you, because your way is perverse before Me."**

In this story, Balaam's donkey sees the angel of the Lord and refuses to move toward him. So even though Balaam physically whips his donkey on three occasions to get back on the road, he refuses to walk toward this angel. Further, we are not told why the donkey won't approach this angel. Yet the donkey senses something supernatural about this angel. Also, nowhere in this story are we told of God opening the eyes of the donkey to see this angel. In contrast, God opened the eyes of Balaam to see the angel of the Lord. As a result, Balaam falls to the ground in fear.

The main spiritual point in this story is Balaam's disobedience toward God. As a result, God sends the angel of the Lord to block Balaam from traveling with the Moabites contingent. Despite this, Balaam cannot see this angel blocking his path, but his donkey does. The fact that Balaam cannot see this angel is not unusual since angels and demons are invisible. What is unusual is that his donkey saw this angel. Yet the donkey does not run away in fear because of it. Instead, the donkey just refuses to move past the angel.

In Scripture, when there is a literal interpretation in a passage you accept it. Whereas if there is symbolic or figurative language used in a passage, you determine the literal interpretation for it. Given this, Balaam's donkey saw an angel, and there is nothing in the Book of Numbers to suggest this donkey was special. If this donkey was not unique, then perhaps animals can detect supernatural things. If so, can animals help us determine the presence of supernatural things?

Few Americans own donkeys today. In contrast, many Americans own dogs or cats, and they have many purposes besides being the family pet. For example, dogs are utilized for hunting, law enforcement, and security. Furthermore, psychologists have found that service dogs are beneficial for veterans suffering from mental health disorders. These service dogs help their owners cope with their disabilities. Sometimes, they save lives by detecting seizures and other physical ailments within individuals. Dogs can do this job because of their sixth sense, which humans do not possess.

If dogs can detect physiological changes within human beings, can they sense the presence of angels and demons? Yes, they can. Unfortunately, this cannot be measured and verified by science. Instead, this comes down to your spiritual discernment. In short, what is the Holy Spirit telling you about the situation? Furthermore, the reactions of your pets toward an individual or something in your home could be confirmation of a dark presence. Reason: animals can sense and see dark entities, which we cannot detect. Given this, your pet's odd behavior could be a physical sign of something demonic.

Although all pet's mannerisms are unique, a common reaction for dogs that detect a dark presence is to bark. In contrast, cats tend to stare intently. Further, your pet's odd behavior will continue until the presence leaves or until their owners intervene. I have observed this odd behavior in my pets and heard similar accounts from family members and friends. Conversely, I have never heard an account of a pet fleeing its home after detecting something demonic. Animals don't flee their homes because they don't fear demons. Instead, they just respond to them.

In summation, the reaction of your pet toward a presence may confirm what you suspect in your spirit. So you must discern what the Holy Spirit is telling you about the situation. Conversely, if you don't get confirmation from the Holy Spirit about the situation, then you pray until God provides an answer. Remember, God knows your spiritual strengths and weaknesses. So, you must trust God unconditionally when trying to detect the presence of demons. Conversely, you don't give in to fear about the situation. Instead, you cite Scripture and ask the Holy Spirit to provide you peace.

Chapter 4

The Lessons of Job

Many people believe the Book of Job is about suffering and how we respond to it. Whereas others contend it's about faith and trust in God when bad things happen to us. Yet there is a third lesson in the Book of Job. That lesson concerns the war between God and Satan. Although many theologians focus on Job's unjust suffering, they don't focus on Satan as the cause for it. Instead, they emphasize Job's bewilderment about his situation and the opinions of his friends.

In Job 1:6–12, we get the backdrop for Job's suffering: **Now there was a day when the sons of God came to present themselves before the Lord, and Satan also came among them. And the Lord said to Satan, "From where do you come?" So Satan answered the Lord and said, "From going to and fro on the earth, and from walking back and forth on it." Then the Lord said to Satan, "Have you considered My servant Job, that there is none like him on the earth, a blameless and upright man, one who fears God and shuns evil?" So Satan answered the Lord and said, "Does Job fear God for nothing? Have You not made a hedge around him, around his household, and around all that he has on every side? You have blessed the work of his hands, and his possessions have increased in the land. But now, stretch out Your hand and touch all that he has, and he will surely curse You to your face." And the Lord said to Satan, "Behold, all that he has is in your power; only do not lay a hand on his person." So Satan went out from the presence of the Lord.**

The first part of this passage is about Satan and his relationship with God. One would think since Satan caused the fall of mankind and led an uprising in Heaven, God would terminate any contact with him. Instead, God still allows him access to Heaven and a platform to voice his opinion. So why would God grant an unworthy privilege to his archenemy whose actions destroyed his original plan for mankind? Because in many ways, God's interaction with Satan puzzles us. As does Job's suffering to prove a point to Satan.

The next point to consider in Job 1:6–12 concerns Satan's activity in the world. Although God knows what Satan is doing in the world, he still queries him about his activity. Yet Satan's actions are meant to deceive, kill, and destroy people. Still, God does not chastise him. Instead, God seems to accept (not like) what Satan does throughout the world. This seems to support the spiritual tenet of free will. So despite the fall of mankind due to freewill, God still allows us to choose. Likewise, God gave angels free will too, which includes Satan.

Although we know Satan loses in the end, he is still allowed to deceive and torment mankind until the last days. As a result, millions of people will be deceived by Satan and spend eternity in Hell. Granted, Satan's deception does not condemn people to Hell, but their rejection of God's gift of salvation through Jesus Christ does. Thus, those who believe the lies of the devil and refuse to accept Christ as Savior cannot blame anyone for their fate. Even though Satan fools many via manipulation and deception. Still, his influence cannot circumvent the power of the Holy Spirit to convict people of their sins and need for a savior.

Even though Satan can deceive and torment people, God has restricted his authority to harm Christians-- although he can hinder and oppress them. This should encourage all Christians to be fearless toward the things of God. Likewise, there are verses in the New Testament that confirm God's hedge of protection over us. For example, in Romans 8:31 there is a short but powerful verse to encourage all believers: **What then shall we say to these things? If God is for us, who can be against us?** Furthermore, we find in 1 John 4:4 clear confirmation that we have authority over the devil: **You are of God, little children, and have overcome them, because He who is in you is greater than he who is in the world.**

Although these verses can strengthen us during difficult times, they don't promise us a pain-free life. Yes, God has placed a hedge of protection over his people, but we still live in a fallen world. A world filled with evil and danger everywhere. As such, we will experience trials and hardships in this world. For example, our physical bodies are vulnerable to disease and the aging process. So as we experience declining health, we must trust God despite our situation. Given this, daily discernment is the key to living a productive Christian life.

We then must ask the question what is God's lesson for us in the Book of Job? We find in Isaiah 55:8–9 a statement from God about his ways: **"For My thoughts are not your thoughts, Nor are your ways My ways," says the Lord. "For as the heavens are higher than the earth, So are My ways higher than your ways, And my thoughts than your thoughts.** These two verses are profound but clear. So even though we don't understand God's rationale for Job's suffering, we must accept it.

Satan Attacks Job

We also find in Job 1:6-12, Satan's contention that Job's faithfulness is due to God's blessings over him and not based on real faith. As a result, Satan dares God to take away his blessings. Satan believes Job will curse God if he does. God does not defend Job's faithfulness against Satan. Instead, he gives Satan permission to take Job's possessions, which include his ten children. This is recorded in Job 1:13–22: **Now there was a day when his sons and daughters were eating and drinking wine in their oldest brother's house; and a messenger came to Job and said, "The oxen were plowing and the donkeys feeding beside them, "when the Sabeans' raided them and took them away—indeed they have killed the servants with the edge of the sword; and I alone have escaped to tell you!" While he was still speaking, another also came and said, "The fire of God fell from heaven and burned up the sheep and the servants, and consumed them; and I alone have escaped to tell you!" While he was still speaking, another also came and said, "The Chaldeans formed three bands, raided the camels and took them away, yes, and killed the servants with the edge of the sword; and I alone have escaped to tell you!" While he was still speaking, another also came and said, "Your sons and daughters were eating and drinking wine in their oldest brother's house, "and suddenly a great wind came from across the wilderness and struck the four corners of the house, and it fell on the young people, and they are dead; and I alone have escaped to tell you!" Then Job arose, tore his** robe, and shaved his head; and he fell to the ground and worshipped. And he said: "Naked I came from my mother's womb, And naked shall I return there. The Lord gave, and the Lord has taken away; Blessed be the name of the Lord." In all this Job did not sin nor charge God with wrong.

This passage shows Satan has the power to control people, and the weather, and cause supernatural events. God did not give Satan this power just to torment Job, he already had this power to do bad things against people! The only thing God did was to lift his hedge of protection off Job. Even then, God said Satan could not touch Job's body just his possessions. Hence, this confirms believers can trust God for protection from evil. Likewise, this passage dispels the notion that Satan is a toothless tiger. Instead, he is evil and hates mankind.

God has restricted Satan's authority to torment believers. So unlike what Job endured, God does not select certain faithful believers today for special torment by the devil. Instead, the story of Job, like Paul of the New Testament, are examples for us to meditate on during difficult times. Although Job was more vocal about his torment than Paul. In both cases, these men experienced superhuman suffering. None of us would want to experience the suffering that Job and Paul endured. Yet we all experience hardships in the world. Therefore, these stories of suffering are to inspire and encourage us to trust God during difficult times.

The authority Satan has (due to the fall of mankind in the garden) to inflict suffering on mankind cannot be dismissed. Furthermore, Satan is not a little devil on your shoulders whispering bad thoughts. Conversely, he is extremely evil. His purpose has been outlined for us in John 10:10: **The thief does not come except to steal, and to kill, and to destroy. I have come that they may have life, and that they may have it more abundantly.** This verse is clear that without salvation through Jesus Christ, we are dead spiritually and subject to the attacks of the devil.

Satan's attacks against Job reveal his nature and what he can do if unrestrained. So even though Job was not disobedient toward God in any way, God used him to show us what Satan can do if unrestrained. Although theologians downplay Satan's role in the Book of Job, no doubt his actions against Job were meant to show us something. Satan's actions against Job were meant to show us God's divine protection. If so, was that fair to Job? Although we may question this, it's not our place to question God. Instead, we should be thankful that God shows us through Job the consequences of Satan's wrath without his hedge of protection.

Second Wave

If the story of Job ended after chapter 1, we would be left wondering why. In short, was Job just a pawn to prove a point to Satan? Furthermore, if Job's story ended with him in despair after losing everything this would conflict with biblical tenets of obedience and faith in God. Fortunately, Job's story does not end in chapter 1, and neither does his suffering. So despite losing everything, Job must endure more attacks from Satan. In Job 2:1–10, we are told about Satan's next strike against Job: **Again there was a day when the sons of God came to present themselves before the Lord, and Satan came also among them to present himself before the Lord. And the Lord said to Satan, "From where do you come?" So Satan answered the Lord and said, "From going to and fro on the earth, and from walking back and forth on it." Then the Lord said to Satan, "Have you considered My servant Job, that there is none like him on the earth, a blameless and upright man, one who fears God and shuns evil? And still holds fast to his integrity, although you incited Me against him, to destroy him without cause." So Satan answered the Lord and said, Skin for skin! Yes, all that a man has he will give for his life. But stretch out your hand now, and touch his bone and his flesh, and he will surely curse you to your face! And the Lord said to Satan, Behold, he is in your hand, but spare his life. So Satan went out from the presence of the Lord, and struck Job with painful boils from the sole of his foot to the crown of his head. And he took for himself a potsherd with which to scrape himself while he sat in the midst of the ashes. Then his wife said to him, Do you still hold fast to your integrity? Curse God and die! But he said to her, You speak as one of the foolish woman speaks. Shall we indeed accept good from God, and shall we not accept adversity? In all this Job did not sin with his lips.**

There is a lot to digest in this passage. The first point concerns this interaction between God and Satan. Again, God knows what Satan is up to, yet he still queries Satan about his activity. Likewise, we get the same response from Satan. Thereafter, God brags about Job's integrity and obedience, but Satan says Job will curse God if his health is taken away. Although God knows Job won't curse him, he still allows Satan to attack him anyway under one condition: he cannot kill Job.

These verses bolster the point that Job's story is about suffering. Likewise, these verses confirm Satan has an agenda. Also, these verses provide us with an insight into God's disposition. A disposition that is hard for us to understand. For instance, God has the same dialogue with Satan as he did in Chapter 1. Why? Because in many ways, God's tone toward Satan seems almost parental. Furthermore, it appears God wants to show Satan something through Job's suffering. If true, is there a lesson for us too?

This passage also provides us with an insight into Job's disposition. For example, when Job's wife tells him to curse God and die, he tells her "Shall we indeed accept good from God, and shall we not accept adversity?" In all this, Job did not sin with his lips. In many ways, Job's disposition is hard to grasp. Yes, it's an illustration of great faith in God. Still, this type of faith seems irrational. It is irrational because few people view adversity from a spiritual perspective. Given this, are we to emulate Job's disposition when facing adversity?

Job's Friends

The next stage of Job's suffering involves accusations from his friends. Even though at first, we get the impression Job has good friends. In Job 2:11–13, we are told about Job's friends: **Now when Job's three friends heard of all this adversity that had come upon him, each one came from his own place—Eliphaz the Temanite, Bildad the Shuhite, and Zophar the Naamathite. For they had made an appointment together to come and mourn with him, and to comfort him. And when they raised their eyes from afar, and did not recognize him, they lifted their voices and wept; and each one tore his robe and sprinkled dust on his head toward heaven. So they sat down with him on the ground seven days and seven nights, and no one spoke a word to him, for they saw that his grief was very great.**

At first glance, it appears Job has strong friends who can comfort him, but this would change. As a result, Job's friends become his critics. The first accusation comes from Eliphaz. He contends Job has sinned and is suffering the consequences. Yet Job insists he has done nothing wrong. The next accusation comes from Bildad. He contends Job should repent. Yet Job responds by citing the power of God and how useless man's efforts are to be righteous. After this exchange, his third friend, Zophar tells Job to repent. Thereafter, Job fires back at his friends for criticizing him and mounts his defense. Throughout these exchanges with his friends, Job proclaims his innocence. The tone of the book then changes in Chapter 32, when a young man named Elihu, decides to speak up.

In Job 32:1–5, Elihu speaks to Job and his friends: **So these three men ceased answering Job, because he was righteous in his own eyes. Then the wrath of Elihu, the son of Barachel the Buzite, of the family of Ram, was aroused against Job; his wrath was aroused because he justified himself rather than God. Also against his three friends his wrath was aroused, because they had found no answer, and yet had condemned Job. Now because they were years older than he, Elihu had waited to speak to Job. When Elihu saw that there was no answer in the mouth of these three men, his wrath was aroused.**

There are two spiritual messages in this passage. One concerns Job, and the other concerns his friends. The first message concerns Job's righteousness. Although Job was the most righteous man on the earth, Elihu contends his righteousness compared to God's is nothing. Given this, Job should have focused on God's purposes behind his suffering rather than proclaiming his innocence of any wrongdoing. Whereas his friends should have stopped accusing Job of wrongdoing and offered their support instead.

By accusing Job of wrongdoing, his friends aggravated the situation and prolonged Job's suffering. As a result, Job reacted to their accusations instead of focusing on God for answers. Perhaps if his friends supported him during this ordeal, the story of Job would have ended sooner. Although Job is awarded in the end by God, he could have been spared Elihu's commentaries about his shortfalls and those of his friends. Likewise, he could have been spared God's subsequent judgment against him.

After Elihu addresses Job and his friends, he then proclaims God's justice, goodness, and majesty, while condemning self-righteousness. No doubt Job and his friends were humbled by Elihu's wisdom and boldness. As a result, after Elihu finishes his commentaries, Job and his friends say nothing to defend themselves. Immediately thereafter, God addresses Job out of a whirlwind but says nothing about Elihu's comments or commentaries. Instead, he immediately attacks Job.

In chapter 38:1–11, God begins to chastise Job: **Then the Lord answered Job out of the whirlwind, and said: "Who is this who darkens counsel By words without knowledge? Now prepare yourself like a man; I will question you, and you shall answer Me. "Where were you when I laid the foundations of the earth? Tell Me, if you have understanding. Who determined its measurements? Surely you know! Or who stretched the line upon it? To what were its foundations fastened? Or who laid its cornerstone, When the morning stars sang together, And all the sons of God shouted for joy? "Or who shut in the sea with doors, When it burst forth and issued from the womb; When I made the clouds its garment, And thick darkness its swaddling band; When I fixed My limit for it, And set bars and doors; When I said, 'This far you may come, but no farther, And here your proud waves must stop!''**

If Job's chastisement ended with these eleven verses, God's majesty could not be questioned. Yet God does not stop here. Instead, God continues to fire off questions to Job while revealing his omnipresence throughout chapters 38, 39, 40, and 41. So it's clear God's spiritual points to Job concerns his sovereignty, majesty, omnipresence, and omnipotence—points that neither Job nor mankind can dispute or challenge. So despite Job's belief and obedience to him—he is not worthy to question God. Likewise, if Job cannot question God—neither can we.

We are given an insight into God's anger in Job 40:1–2: **Moreover, the Lord answered Job, and said, "Shall the one who contends with the Almighty correct God, let him answer it."** Later, in Job 40:7–8, God tells us why he is angry toward Job: **"Now prepare yourself like a man; I will question you, and you shall answer Me: "Would you indeed annul My judgment? Would you condemn Me that you may**

be justified?" Job has no defense for these charges against him by God. So despite the unbelievable suffering he endured from Satan, God says: You don't question me! That is a powerful statement that applies to us too.

Points to Remember

Job subsequently repents after realizing he cannot question God. As a result, God blesses Job with twice as much as he had before. Some may contend God blessed Job because he repented of his sin. Although it was important for Job to admit he was wrong concerning God's ways, this one act was not the reason God blessed him. Instead, this one act allowed God to bless Job because of his faithfulness and obedience. So this spiritual principle of God awarding faithfulness still applies to believers.

Although the Book of Job is about suffering, it's also a revelation about Satan's agenda and tactics. So unlike the persona presented by our culture, Satan is not a toothless tiger. Instead, he is extremely powerful and the instrument of evil in this world. Furthermore, Satan knows how to attack us based on our spiritual strengths and weaknesses. Despite this, God restricts what Satan can do to believers if they're obedient and living for him. Conversely, when believers choose to live ungodly lifestyles, God's hedge of protection won't apply.

Another lesson in the Book of Job concerns his friends. Job's friends were great men of faith; however, their views about Job's situation were wrong. Like Job, his friends never asked God for discernment on the matter. Instead, they assumed Job did something wrong to warrant his fate. As a result, they did great harm to Job with their accusations. Conversely, Elihu relied on God's Spirit before saying anything about the situation. This is a significant spiritual point that is often missed by Christians when they judge each other.

Chapter 5

Church Denominations

Satan has used many tactics to keep people from getting saved. One of Satan's most effective tactics is division within the church. Even the early church experienced division; however, once all the original apostles died, Christians throughout the Roman Empire started going in different directions. As a result, the Catholic church took control of the faith in the fourth century by suppressing different fractions. Yet after Martin Luther's Protestant Reformation, Christian denominations started forming. This formation of different Christian denominations exploded in the twentieth century.

Although there are many independent churches today, the majority are affiliated with a denomination. Some have estimated the number of Christian denominations at forty thousand, yet the true number is unknown. What we do know is that all denominations and independent churches derived from the original Catholic church and the Protestant Reformation.

For the first thousand years of Christianity, the Catholic church controlled what people were taught. This started changing in the eleventh century as people questioned the authority of the church. The Catholic church, however, fought hard to keep its power and control over kings and believers. As a result, if anyone tried to break away or challenge the Catholic church from the eleventh to the sixteenth century, they lost their position of authority or life. It wasn't until the Protestant Reformation, under Martin Luther, that the power of the Catholic church declined. After Luther, other Christian leaders established different denominations. Yet the key development that weakened the power of the Catholic church and established a template for other Protestant denominations was the printing of the King James Bible in 1611. This Bible allowed every layman access to God's Word.

Church in America

The next great event that shaped denominations was the establishment of colonies in America. For example, the Puritans were the first group of people that came to America for religious freedom. The Puritans were extremely conservative, and they influenced what seventeenth-century Christians in America believed in. In time, though, many of the Puritans' core principles changed to reflect American values of freedom and self-reliance.

In the eighteenth and nineteenth centuries, other immigrants came to America and brought their denominational doctrines too. And like the Puritans, their denominational doctrines changed to reflect American values and principles. As a result, America's melting pot of immigrants also transformed Old World denominations. This transformation of core denominational beliefs is still occurring today.

There is no doubt that the history of the United States was shaped by what American Christians believed in. For example, the American Revolution was about taxes and the king's authority over the colonies. Some churches of the day supported England, while others insisted liberty was a God-given right. Later, the Mexican American War of 1846 was more about a Christian manifest destiny than a suppressive Mexican regime over Texas. Then in 1861, the American Civil War started because at its core was the issue of slavery. The Northern Christians of the day felt that slavery was evil and had to be stopped. Southerners, however, did not share this conviction. Granted, the Civil War started because the South wanted to secede from the Union, but the moral impetus for it was slavery.

In the early twentieth century, the Pacifist movement kept the United States out of World War I until 1917. Likewise, the Temperance Movement pushed Prohibition through Congress in 1919. The people behind these movements strongly believed their positions were biblical. For example, the Pacifists cited Jesus's teachings of nonviolent to support their position against war and killing, whereas members of the Temperance Movement blamed alcohol for all the wrongs in society. These two movements greatly shaped policies and politics before World War II. After World War II, though, the influence of religious movements in shaping American foreign policy ended. As a result, geopolitical forces started dictating American foreign policy after 1945. A change that is still in effect today.

After World War II

The greatest achievement of the church after World War II was the Civil Rights Movement of the 1950s and 1960s. Although black advocates and progressive whites received most of the credit for this movement, black churches played a major role in motivating their members to demand change by using nonviolent methods. This nonviolent approach ultimately changed laws and attitudes about race in the country. As a result, the crowning achievement of this movement was the Civil Rights Act of 1964.

In the 1980s, Jerry Falwell formed the Moral Majority. This organization united many conservative Christian denominations as a political force to address the social issues of the day. Ronald Reagan and the Republican Party benefited greatly from the support of this organization. Sadly, they never delivered any major legislation conservative Christians wanted. This failure, in many ways, discouraged many Christians. As a result, during the 1990s the Moral Majority as a political force faded away. Despite the collapse of the Moral Majority, many conservative Christians still vote Republican today because of their moral positions on abortion and traditional marriage.

Although there are still regions in the country where the spiritual positions of candidates matter, those regions are dwindling. Chiefly because many Christians no longer adhere to the moral positions held by their churches. Many Christians feel this way today because of the negative messages conveyed by the media and our culture. Messages that mock core tenets of Christianity as outdated and irrelevant.

Even though the media is liberal and anti-Christian, they have always opposed the influence of faith in our culture. Granted, our culture has grown liberal too, but that has been the trend throughout the twentieth century, especially after World War II. No doubt these liberal forces have influenced the spiritual condition of the country. Still, the real blame for the decline and power of the church in America is the church.

The Seeds of Change

There were several events during the sixties that changed America and the church: the Vietnam War, the assassinations of political figures, birth control, feminism, and the civil rights demonstrations all influenced our society. Because of these events, many Americans changed their views about government, school prayer, national service, sex, drugs, and traditional roles for women. Then in the seventies, abortions became legal, and divorce laws were eased.

These liberal positions were subsequently passed down to the next generation. This also affected people of faith. The church, however, in the 1970s had no answers for hurting people struggling with divorce, drugs, and promiscuity. Unfortunately, most churches ignored these issues and acted like these problems did not affect Christians. Conversely, some churches continued to preach hell and brimstone sermons concerning these issues. Yet neither approach addressed the needs of hurting Christians, who were struggling with faith and obedience to the Word.

In the 1980s, Jerry Falwell did unite many conservative Christians, but other factions within the church changed how services were conducted. This new trend emphasized prosperity and positive thinking. As a result, many churches subsequently changed the content and tone of their sermons. This new Christian message emphasized the benefits of believing in Christ. Furthermore, the super televangelists of this era dominated Christian television with this new message too. At the height of their popularity in the eighties, millions of Christians watched these televangelists weekly and gave generously to their ministries. Unfortunately, in the late eighties, some of these ministries were rocked by sex scandals. As a result, many televangelists of the time lost followers and financial support.

One lasting effect of the eighties is a divided church. As a result, there is no clear political voice among Christians. This is evident in the voting patterns of Christians: Black and Hispanic Christians vote one way and Whites another. Also, after the 1980s, church membership started to decline. As a result, the percentage of Christians attending church regularly has steadily declined. This decline is especially alarming for children brought up in the church. As a result, throughout the country, church membership is declining, and most churches today are attended by older adults with fewer young people. Thus, young adults have fallen away from the church. This has caused a spiritual void among young adults in the country. As a result, many churches are compromising the gospel to attract new members. Yet these new gospels are not based on Scripture.

False Gospels

A major reason for the decline of church attendance in America is due to false teachings. The Bible warns us not to believe in or practice false gospels. We find in Galatians 1:6–9 a warning from Paul about perverting the gospel: **I marvel that you are turning away so soon from Him who called you in the grace of Christ, to a different gospel, which is not another; but some trouble you and want to pervert the gospel of Christ. But even if we, or an angel from heaven, preach any other gospel to you than what we have preached to you, let him be accursed. As we have said before, so now I say again, if anyone preaches any other gospel to you than what you have received, let him be accursed.**

Given this powerful warning about false gospels, what is the true gospel? The true gospel message is that Jesus Christ came into the world to die for our sins and to restore our relationship with the Father. So Christ is the New Covenant, whereby sinful man has been sanctified. Thereafter, the Christian's mission is to conform to the image of Jesus Christ and spread the Good News. And if one is obedient to live the Christian life, God promises to take care of their needs. Conversely, any doctrine that contradicts this message is a false gospel.

There is nothing wrong with Christians disagreeing on topics of faith if their positions do not contradict the Bible. Conversely, if an individual, pastor, church, or denomination teaches something that violates the Bible, it must be challenged. For example, there have been Christians throughout the history of the church who have done things that harmed the church. Even the early church was guilty of making these mistakes. We find a powerful example of this in Acts 15:37–40: **Now Barnabas was determined to take with them John called Mark. But Paul insisted that they should not take with them the one who had departed from them in Pamphylia, and had not gone with them to the work. Then the contention became so sharp that they parted from one another.**

And so Barnabas took Mark and sailed to Cyprus; but Paul chose Silas and departed, being commended by the brethren to the grace of God.

Paul and Barnabas were the super televangelists of the first-century church. The Bible refers to Paul and Barnabas as anointed to preach the gospel. Yet a disagreement over Mark's faithfulness caused a great division between them. This contention was so sharp they went their separate ways. Paul had his convictions and reasons for feeling this way toward Mark. Likewise, Barnabas did not feel Mark committed the unpardonable sin. Although neither position violated any major biblical tenets, their dispute over it undermined unity in the church.

This disagreement between Paul and Barnabas pales in comparison to what is occurring in the church today. The church today has never had more denominational variations. Granted, some of these denominational differences are minor and not questioning core Christian tenets. Conversely, some churches are preaching messages that conflict with the core tenets of the Bible; moreover, some churches are more concerned with their attendance and entertaining people than preaching the gospel of Jesus Christ.

Although we have liberty in Christ to do all things, we cannot promote or practice things that conflict with the Word. In view of this, if a church at its core is preaching Christ, then how the service is conducted does not matter. If, however, a church has a different emphasis than Christ, you should question it. The basis for testing a church's doctrine is the Bible. Your preference for how a service should be conducted does not matter. What matters is whether the pastor's focus is on Scripture.

The many Christian denominations today have produced confusion within and outside the church. Because of this confusion, nonbelievers cannot get clarity about Christianity. Their choices are no longer just Catholic or Protestant. Even within mainstream Protestant denominations like the Baptist, there are conservative, moderate, and liberal variations. These fractions within denominations are different throughout the country. In short, the church body is divided, and it cannot respond strongly to all the negative forces against it.

Given the numerous denominations and their agendas within Christianity, some critical biblical principles have been ignored by the church. These principles are ignored because they are not well understood or popular today. As a result, God must reveal these principles to the church in different ways. Sometimes, God will use dreams, visions, or words of wisdom to convey spiritual principles to Christians. Some of these principles are as follows:

Self-Denial

Although many Christians have heard the passage "Take up your cross and follow Me," few understand what this means. The life of a Christian is to give up self-gratification to serve God and others. The number one person we serve is God. We serve God by trusting him on all matters of importance: who should I marry? What church should I attend? Where should I work and live? Even faithful Christians make major decisions without waiting on God. For God to truly bless you in all areas, you must wait on him. So asking God to bless your marriage, church, job, or home after the fact is not waiting on God. Although God may still honor your prayers if your decisions have not violated his Word.

Another aspect of self-denial involves God's plan for your life. Many Christians mistakenly believe God is going to force them to do something they don't want to do, such as ministry. They feel this way because the idea of living in a third-world country as missionaries with few amenities terrifies many Christians. Yet God would never force anyone into ministry unless they had a heart for it. A heart for ministry can only come from God. So whatever God calls you to do, he'll prepare you for it. Sometimes that preparation is education, experience, or a combination of both. Furthermore, God will never call you to do something against your will. Granted, as Americans, we are impatient people. So the thought of waiting months or years for God to work out his purpose in our lives is unacceptable. Yet sometimes, though, God will give us a road-to-Damascus revelation like what Paul experienced to change our course.

Christ-Centered Relationship

There are many Christians today who are active in their churches. They could be elders, deacons, or youth pastors. They are sincere and try to live the Christian life, but they do not have a relationship with Jesus

Christ. If true, how is this possible? It is possible because the conviction of the Holy Spirit that brings one to repentance doesn't mean a person has a relationship with Christ. What it means is that that person has the means to establish a relationship with Jesus Christ. You establish a relationship with Christ through your prayer life, reading the Word, and learning to listen to the inner voice of the Holy Spirit.

On the surface, this plan for establishing a relationship with Christ appears easy to do. Conversely, it takes a great deal of faith to carry it out. It takes great faith because adversity from the flesh, the world, and the enemy will come against one after they are saved. Given this, sometimes God will keep adversity away from young Christians until their faith has grown stronger. For example, I experienced this firsthand. God kept me away from serious adversity for the first seven years after my conversion. So during those seven years, I established a routine of worship that saw me through great future trials. Furthermore, if I had not established that daily worship routine during these early years, I would have departed from the faith once adversity came.

For Christians to grow closer to God, they must have a daily commitment to spend time with God. The more time they spend with God, the stronger their faith will become—there is no other way. So whether they are driving to work, at work, or doing mundane tasks at home, they must pray constantly and be receptive to God's presence. No, constant praying is not meaningless chatting, but a constant awareness of God's presence by acknowledging him daily in all things.

The same principles we use to establish good relationships with our spouse, friends, and coworkers apply to God too. In short, you talk, confide, trust, and spend time with God. God should not be viewed as a spiritual taskmaster nor as Santa Claus. Unfortunately, the way you view God is often shaped or taught by the church you attend. So if your church has a distorted view of who or what God is, you'll have the same view.

Although your pastor and church play major roles in your spiritual development, they are not a substitute for your responsibility to know God personally and intimately. The Bible is clear on matters of faith: ask, knock, and seek. So, when you want to know God and not religion, he will show up and never let you go.

Sin of Unforgiveness

Many Christians harbor unforgiveness toward believers and others who have hurt them. Jesus was clear about unforgiveness: it's not acceptable. The Bible says if you don't forgive others neither will your Father in Heaven forgive you. That is a disturbing statement from the creator of the universe. Yet many Christians hold grudges, dislikes, and flat-out unforgiveness toward members of their church. Furthermore, they won't acknowledge these feelings to others, their pastor, or God. As a result, their unconfessed sin toward others opens the door for oppressive spirits of bitterness and unforgiveness, which will destroy their testimony for Christ. Likewise, they will be miserable and have no joy in the Lord.

Like all unconfessed sins in your life, you must confess it to God. The confession is just the first step. Also, you must sincerely want these dark feelings to go away. Likewise, if you have harbored these feelings for years, they are now ingrained in your mind and spirit. If so, there is a good possibility that an oppressive spirit has taken hold of you too. You will know if a dark spirit has taken hold of you because your prayers won't be answered, and you will lose faith and confidence in God. When this occurs, you'll need help from your pastor, elders, deacons, or other spirit-filled Christians who understand spiritual warfare.

Although many churches may preach on forgiveness, they won't elaborate on the consequences for a believer who won't forgive others. Furthermore, your pastor may not understand spiritual warfare. Many mainstream Protestant churches today simply don't teach on controversial subjects such as oppressive spirits. Given this, if you're not a member of an Evangelical church that believes in the gifts of the spirit, you need to find one that does.

Legalism

The Bible has a lot to say about legalism. Jesus was especially critical of the Scribes and Pharisees of his days because they were legalistic. In short, they were consumed by rules and acts that appeared godly, but their hearts were far from God. They were religious but lost. Likewise, there are legalistic Christian churches today. They too believe their religious acts are confirmation of true salvation, and there is no compromise. For example, these types of churches believe if one ever drinks alcohol, gets divorced, does not attend church weekly, or fails to read their Bible daily they are not saved.

There are fewer of these types of churches today compared to the past. Still, what we have today is denominational legalism. These denominations may not preach other Christians are lost, but they will imply others lack biblical authority. For example, I have been baptized four times. The reason I was given by these churches was because other denominations lacked biblical authority to baptize me. Yet Scripture is clear that any born-again Christian can baptize one.

Another prevalent legalistic belief practiced by many conservative denominations is skepticism about the Charismatic movement. Yet despite this skepticism by conservative denominations, most adults who are coming to Christ are members of Charismatic churches. This should encourage all Christians that Americans are still coming to Christ. Unfortunately, this is not the case. Instead, there is resentment within the ranks of many Protestant denominations that the Charismatic movement has hijacked Christianity.

The main disagreement many Protestant denominations have about Charismatics is that they doubt the baptism of the Holy Spirit. In short, they contend laying hands on the sick, casting out demons, speaking in tongues, and receiving visions or prophecies ended with the apostles. Although most Protestant Christians feel Charismatics are saved, they doubt their gifts. Also, some conservative denominations believe the Charismatic Movement is a false gospel.

The Bible is clear there will be differences and disagreements among Christians. The church is often referred to as the Body of Christ. So just like our body, not all parts serve the same purpose, but all are necessary. This debate concerning the baptism of the Holy Spirit should not divide the church. Therefore, mainstream Protestants need to accept Charismatics as members of the Body. Likewise, Charismatics need to stop insisting that all Christians must be baptized in the Spirit.

As Christians, we must follow Jesus's main command: love one another. So even if you don't understand or accept what other Christians believe in, they are your brothers and sisters in Christ. Thus, you must view all Christians as your extended family. So one day, you'll be in Heaven with Christians from various backgrounds and denominations.

When that day comes, it won't matter what denomination or church they once attended.

Chapter 6

Born-Again Deception

The most popular passage in the New Testament is John 3:16: **For God so loved the world that He gave His only begotten Son, that whoever believes in Him should not perish but have everlasting life.** Many nonbelievers are familiar with this verse too. Since they have seen it displayed on billboards, signs, and in television commercials. Likewise, pastors often cite it as God's plan for salvation. The keyword in this verse is *believe*. Yet the Greek meaning for *believe* does not translate well into English.

The Greek word for *believe* is *pistueo*, which means "to trust in and rely upon," "commit to the charge of," "confide in," or "have a mental persuasion." Given this, if we change John 3:16 to reflect this meaning, the passage changes to "For God so loved the world that He gave His only begotten Son, that whoever trusts in and rely upon, commit to the charge of, confide in, have a mental persuasion in Him should not perish but have everlasting life," the entire focus of the verse changes. The verse now focuses on total faith and commitment to Jesus Christ for salvation. A commitment to God that is not easy. Instead, it requires true repentance.

If a true commitment to Jesus Christ requires a radical change in one's life, then why aren't pastors preaching this message? Instead, the salvation prayer is their focus: Dear God, I know I'm a sinner. I ask for your forgiveness. I believe Jesus Christ is your Son. I believe that he died for my sins and that you raised him to life. I want to trust him as my Savior and follow him as Lord from this day forward. Guide my life and help me to do your will. I pray this in the name of Jesus. Amen.

The salvation prayer is part of the process of getting saved, and pastors cite many verses to explain why a person must confess Christ. One popular salvation verse is Romans 10:9: **That if you confess with your mouth the Lord Jesus and believe in your heart that God has raised Him from the dead, you will be saved.** Despite this verse, many people believe they are good. Thus, they contend why do I have to admit I am a sinner? The biblical response to this argument is Romans 6:23: **For the wages of sin is death, but the gift of God is eternal life in Christ Jesus our Lord.**

Most Protestant denominations believe a person must confess Christ to be saved. This is a biblical tenet that few Protestant denominations dispute. What is not biblical is how some televangelists and churches proclaim this tenet. Although they contend one must confess Christ, how that confession is made has changed. For instance, a public confession of going forward for prayer is no longer required. Instead, people are told to just say this little prayer and you're saved. This is how many pastors interpret Romans 10:9.

Although a confession prayer is the first step toward salvation, true repentance and commitment to Jesus Christ require more than an acknowledgment of one's sinfulness. Yet many churches fail to follow up with new believers. As a result, many of these individuals abandon their faith and resume their old lifestyle. Although true salvation is an individual responsibility, the church is responsible for disciplining new believers. When they fail to do this, Satan wins.

The Parable of the Sower

Throughout the New Testament, the question of salvation was addressed many times. The Bible is clear on this matter: Believe in the Lord Jesus Christ and you'll be saved. Further, once an individual accepts Christ, they are to be baptized. Although there is some disagreement among Christians about the purpose of baptism, it's not necessary for salvation. Instead, baptism is an outward action to confirm an inward decision. Furthermore, if Jesus thought it was important to be baptized, then it applies to us too.

Although the Bible proclaims belief in the Lord Jesus Christ for salvation, a saved individual must demonstrate signs of a true believer. The strongest passage in the Bible to support this position is the parable of the sower. In Mark 4:2–9, Jesus explains who is saved and the evidence to prove it: **Then He taught them many things by parables, and said to them His teaching: "Listen! Behold, a sower went out to sow. "And it happened, as he sowed, that some seed fell by the wayside; and the birds of the air came and devoured it. "Some fell on stony ground, where it did not have much earth; and immediately it sprang up because it had no depth of earth. "But when the sun was up it was scorched, and because it had no root it withered away. "And some seed fell among thorns; and the thorns grew up and choked it, and it yielded no crop."But other seed fell on good ground and yielded a crop that sprang up, increased and produced: some thirtyfold, some sixty, and some a hundred." And He said to them, "He who has ears to hear, let him hear."**

In Mark 4:13–20, Jesus tells his apostles the interpretation: **And He said to them, "Do you not understand this parable? How then will you understand all the parables? "The sower sows the word. "And these are the ones by the wayside where the word is sown. When they hear, Satan comes immediately and takes away the word that was sown in their hearts. "These likewise are the ones sown on stony ground who, when they hear the word, immediately receive it with gladness; "and they have no root in themselves, and so endure only for a time. Afterward, when tribulation or persecution arises for the word's sake, immediately they stumble. "Now these are the ones sown among thorns; they are the ones who hear the word, "and the cares of this world, the deceitfulness of riches, and the desires for other things entering in choke the word, and it becomes unfruitful. "But these are the ones sown on good ground, those who hear the word, accept it, and bear fruit: some thirtyfold, some sixty, and some a hundred."**

Based on Jesus's parable, it's clear that true salvation must be a spiritual transformation that changes how one thinks, acts, and believes. Although confessing Christ and repenting for one's sins is the first step toward salvation, it's only the first step. After that, one must show their decision for Christ was life changing. Even strong believers will face times when they question God, but they never doubt he exists. Given this, if a new believer refuses to reject Christ after experiencing criticism and persecution this proves one's salvation is genuine.

Although only God knows who is truly saved, a true believer will show signs of genuine faith. No doubt Jesus would agree with this assessment. Jesus would agree with this assessment because the spiritual points from the parable of the sower have not changed. Furthermore, Satan has many ways to deceive and snatch away faith from new believers today. This is why new believers must be prepared for the attacks of the devil. Unfortunately, like in our country, the church is divided and has different agendas. Yet discipleship for new believers is not an agenda pursued by many churches. As a result, the lack of discipleship by churches is the main reason new believers fall away from their faith. Thus, they never learn how to listen to the voice of the Holy Spirit.

Holy Spirit

Many Christians do not understand the purpose of the Holy Spirit. Likewise, many pastors don't emphasize the importance of the Holy Spirit. Although Jesus's death on the cross started Christianity, it's the Holy Spirit that convicts people of sin and the need for a savior. So without the urgings of the Holy Spirit, a nonbeliever will never accept Christ. Once they accept Christ, the Holy Spirit enters their heart. Given this, if one has truly been saved, they will yield to the inner voice of the Holy Spirit.

Churches can differ in how they conduct their services based on many factors. Yet if a church is not attended by true believers in Jesus Christ who are indwelled with the Holy Spirit, their works won't save people. Their works won't save people because God rejects religious works as a substitute for Jesus. Only Jesus is the propitiation for our sins, and nothing else saves people. In addition, only the works of saved individuals indwelled by the Holy Spirit can draw people to Christ. Given this, a body of believers must listen to what the Holy Spirit is saying about the work they should be doing.

Although many people have opinions regarding true salvation in Jesus Christ, the Bible mentions three characteristics of saved individuals: First, they have unshakable faith in Jesus Christ. Secondly, they are indwelled by the Holy Spirit. Thirdly, they produce fruit for the Lord. Biblical fruit are works or acts done for the Lord prompted by the Holy Spirit. In contrast, involvement with church activities not inspired by the Holy Spirit is not biblical fruit.

False Salvation

Perhaps the most disturbing passage in the Bible is Matthew 7:19–23. In this passage, Jesus talks about religious people who are lost: **Every tree that does not bear good fruit is cut down and thrown into the fire. Therefore by their fruits you will know them. "Not everyone who says to Me, Lord, Lord, shall enter the kingdom of heaven, but he who does the will of My Father in heaven. Many will say to Me in that day, 'Lord, Lord, have we not prophesied in Your name, cast out demons in Your name, and done many wonders in Your name?' And then I will declare to them, 'I never knew you; depart from Me, you who practice lawlessness!"**

Even though Jesus was speaking to a Jewish audience, this passage refers to churchgoers who believe they're saved. They believe they're saved due to their prophesying, casting out demons, and doing good deeds in Jesus's name. In short, they're doing religious works. Yet despite these good works, Jesus will tell these people, "I never knew you." Instead, Jesus says, You must do the will of my Father in Heaven. Given this, what is the will of my Father in Heaven? Because based on Jesus's declaration, religious acts won't save a person. Instead, we find in Ephesians 2:8–9 verses that confirm it's God's grace that saves one, not works: **For by grace you have been saved through faith, and that not of yourself; it is the gift of God, not of works, lest anyone should boast.**

Given this verse, along with Jesus's warning in Matthew 7:19–23, what is the will of God? The first thing one must do is confess Jesus as savior; however, the basis for this confession must be a willingness to repent. The Greek meaning for *repent* is "to have a transformation of heart, a spiritual conversion," "to include a repudiation of self and changed mind." Yes, confessing Christ verbally is necessary, but there must be an internal change too. This change won't occur overnight; however, if one has truly been saved, one will show signs of true repentance.

Another aspect of true conversion is a desire to get involved with a church. If Christ is in you, you will have a desire to be around other believers. So the excuse that people in the church are hypocrites won't fly with God. If you have this view a spiritual inventory is necessary;

moreover, if that is true of the church you're attending—find another church. Also, even though church attendance and involvement will strengthen you, it's only part of your relationship with Jesus Christ. You must also read your Bible and pray daily.

The Holy Spirit is also part of a true salvation conversion. Although there is some dispute among Christians about the role of the Holy Spirit, believers must learn how to discern his voice. I say *voice* because the Holy Spirit is not some mysterious force in the world. Instead, it's a person like Jesus, who resides inside us. The difference, though, is that the Holy Spirit can be suppressed or ignored by believers. Unfortunately, many believers have never learned how to discern the urges of the Holy Spirit. As a result, they rob themselves of an intimate relationship with God.

Many Christians fail to be receptive to the urging of the Holy Spirit. Yes, they may truly be saved, but they are missing out on a great comforter. The Word says to ask, knock, and seek. Although this verse is often cited by pastors for requesting things from God, it also applies to knowing God intimately via the Holy Spirit. Given the importance of the Holy Spirit, believers must learn to hear his voice. Likewise, if believers have unresolved sin in their life this will block the voice of the Holy Spirit.

A truly saved individual will also be transformed. This transformation concerns how one thinks and one's desires. Sadly, many Christians are reluctant to give up their free will. Mainly because they believe God is going to force them to do something against their will—like becoming a missionary in a third-world country. The truth is God never forces anyone to do anything against their will. Also, God only expects you to do the work associated with your gifting. Thus, if you cannot sing, he won't force you to join the choir.

This spiritual transformation does not occur overnight. It's a process that takes time. Although there are individuals called to ministry early in life, most Christians must be prepared to do God's work. Sometimes this preparation only requires education and mentorship. Conversely, sometimes one must undergo many trials before they're receptive to the Lord's calling for their life. Given this, when you have a sense of peace in your heart and a passion for what you're doing for the Lord, you've achieved your calling.

Summation

To resist the world, flesh, and the enemy one must truly be saved. True salvation can only occur if a person repents of their old lifestyle and desires to live a Christian life. This requires the indwelling of the Holy Spirit. Without the Holy Spirit, one's sinful nature cannot be controlled. Thereafter, once a person learns to yield to the urgings of the Holy Spirit, they will produce works for the Lord. Conversely, just performing religious works for a church without the presence of the Holy Spirit won't save people.

The Bible says by their fruit you will know them. If you're truly saved, people will know. They will see a difference in how you talk, act, and respond to difficult situations. Yes, we all fall short in many areas; however, genuine Christians do not resort to the measures of the world when facing adversity. Likewise, you'll sense something different about their persona. A persona that is different from people of the world. If that is the way people view you, your salvation is true. The problem is we have an adversary. His name is Satan.

Although Jesus defeated him on the cross two thousand years ago, one must be saved to exercise the authority they have to confront Satan and his demons. Even after one is saved, the devil will use whatever he can to keep that believer frustrated and oppressed. The devil will use false teachings, generational curses, and past personal sins to keep one spinning in an endless circle. Therefore, believers need to attend churches that equip them for spiritual warfare. In short, knowing how to interpret the schemes of the devil and how to apply the Word to situations.

Chapter 7

Final Thoughts

When I was a junior in high school, I took a philosophy course. One day, the philosophy teacher asked us to write a question on the chalkboard. We were told that no matter what we asked our questions would be answered. I asked: What faith is the right one? Once we wrote our questions on the board, the teacher then asked us to comment on the questions. One girl thought my question missed the mark. She believed any faith in God was good enough, and it did not matter the religion. I did not try to defend my question; however, I knew she missed the point of my question.

After the questions were debated, the teacher told us he'd asked who or what was the source for the answers to these questions. Only one student in the class shared the teacher's reasoning. Granted, as teenagers, we lack the experience of living as adults in the world, which can provide valuable insight into life. So no doubt if this teacher called us back to his class today, most of us would have asked: who or what is the source for the answers to our questions?

Wisdom

The Bible cites wisdom as something that is precious and should be pursued. Unfortunately, most wisdom comes from learning from the mistakes or regrets of our past. For example, when I was an Army recruiter, every adult I spoke to who served in the military told me the same thing: I wish I would have stayed in for twenty years. They felt that way now because serving in the military for twenty years would have earned them an instant retirement.

Although there are a few issues in the world that most could agree upon, the wisdom of hindsight about one's wrong choices in life would be one of them. We ponder if only this or that decision, my life could have turned out differently—so we think. And though we try our best to teach our kids not to make our mistakes, many times they do. If not, they make their own mistakes. So despite what mistakes we make in life, we learn from them.

So often our experiences in life provide us wisdom for the future. That wisdom could be the types of jobs we pursue, a compatible spouse, finances, or where we live. Likewise, our Christian journey provides us worldly wisdom too, but also valuable spiritual insight. An experienced Christian knows adversity will come, but they also know God is with them through it. As such, they can be a tremendous source of strength for those who need encouragement.

I have always believed most Christian men not in ministry do not get serious about God until their forties. The reason: Men first pursue the things the world thinks are important. We are told to get our education, establish our career, and sow our wild oats while we're young, then marry and settle down. Likewise, the church conveys a similar message. The church, though, should be emphasizing a different message. That message is God has a plan for your life. If you know that plan, then everything else falls into place. Unfortunately, most Christian men waste years pursuing the things of the world but ignore God's plan for their life.

The truth is that many Christians do not know God's plan for their life, but neither do they want to know it. As a result, only after tragedy hits will some Christians change course and decide to trust God. Conversely, some Christians never change and just blame God for all their disappointments in life. Yet if one never comes to the saving grace of Jesus Christ, one will not spend eternity with him.

God's Ways

If God knows most Christians will get sidetracked in life, why doesn't he simply intervene? Every Christian that has ever lived has at some point in their life asked this question: Why, God? Why, God did my spouse die of cancer? Why, God did I lose my child? Why, God can't I get ahead with my finances? The why questions are endless. If God is all-powerful and all knowing, then why does he allow his children to experience hardship and pain? So although it's important to establish a relationship with God that is personal, intimate, and continuous, we must remember that God is God. And the ways of God are not our ways. In Isaiah 55:8–9 this is spelled out for us: **"For My thoughts are not your thoughts, Nor are your ways My ways," says the Lord. "For as the heavens are higher than the earth, So are My ways higher than your ways, And My thoughts than your thoughts."**

These verses are simplistic but profound. Perhaps when we go to church or associate with other Christians, we acknowledge the awesomeness of God when things are good. Yet when tragedy hits our family or us, do we just say the right things publicly, but down deep we are angry, bitter, and disillusioned with God. We may even be angry enough with God to tell him off or doubt that he cares for us. I felt this way once towards God, but it only lasted six months. Despite this attitude on my part, God did reveal why my business failed. As a result, I changed my priorities in life and put my family first.

Many nonbelievers doubt the existence of God because of all the suffering and perceived wrongs in the world. They argue if God is all-powerful, knowing, and loving why doesn't he do something about the evil in the world? As a Christian, you may try to explain to a nonbeliever about original sin and the consequences for mankind because of it. Likewise, you may try to explain there is evil in the world because of Satan and his demons. Although you know these things to be true based on Scripture, how do you respond when nonbelievers question your faith, character, and reasoning?

God Focus

Whether we've experienced a great deal of suffering in life or just can't figure it out, the right focus is critical. If we feel that God's purpose is to make us happy and prosperous, we won't respond well to adversity. Likewise, if we feel God wants total obedience or else chastisement will come, then we live by fear and not by grace. Still, God is holy, and expects his children to live right, but he knows we cannot do it without the Holy Spirit. Although all believers have the Holy Spirit inside of them, he will never overrule your free will. Thus, if you don't want to live for God, you can and will block the inner voice of the Holy Spirit.

We find in Malachi 3:6 a statement from God: **"For I am the Lord, I do not change; Therefore you are not consumed, O sons of Jacob."**

Some pastors may argue that God was speaking to the Jews and not to Christians. No, God was speaking to his children at that time in history. Like Israel of the Old Testament, the church today is falling away from God. Furthermore, many Christian denominations and churches are trying to reinvent the gospel of Jesus Christ. The gospel of Jesus Christ is not about prosperity, entertainment, or being happy. The gospel is about accepting Christ and conforming to his image.

For many American Christians to conform to the image of Jesus Christ, they must change how they think, act, and believe. This can only happen when God's Spirit descends on the church through revival. God will bring revival to America because it's the heart of Christianity in the world. Thus, if God fixes the heart of the problem in the church, then all its members throughout the world will be revived as well. Given this, every Christian who wants revival must be willing to receive it.

Christians are not cattle, but individuals. Therefore, God will deal with us as individuals. He will design a series of steps to correct how one thinks, acts, and believes. Sometimes, though, God will intervene in one's life immediately. For example, if one is addicted to drugs or alcohol, God may remove that addiction instantly. Still, the root causes for that addiction will have to be addressed by the individual too. Conversely, if that individual won't change course, God will never overrule their free will.

There is no standard blueprint for how God will accomplish his purposes for one's life. A lot will depend on where that individual is spiritually and where they are supposed to be. Likewise, a lot will depend on the plans God has for one. For example, the level of faith and obedience for a pastor must be higher than that of a church member assigned to the choir. Although all must conform to the image of Christ. No, the pastor is not more precious to God than the choir member. He just has more responsibilities. As such, his level of spirituality must be higher than Christians not in ministry.

On a personal note, I came from a non-Christian home. Although I was saved at twenty, I did not fully understand the Bible. As a result, what churches I attended influenced how I interpreted Scripture. For many years, I grew little spiritually; however, after going through a series of life-changing events, I was receptive to viewing Scripture in a different light. One aspect of that light was receiving the gifts of the Holy Spirit. Another aspect of that light concerned spiritual warfare. In short, the Lord showed me how Satan used my past to keep me suppressed. Satan suppressed me due to past emotional wounds, and family generational curses. As a result, only after I received the baptism of the Holy Spirit was I able to overcome the demonic forces against me.

My Christian journey is not unique. All Christians must battle the world, flesh, and Satan. What many believers fail to realize is that Satan wants to destroy their testimony for Christ. Furthermore, if God allows it, he will try to kill you. Granted, we have God's hedge of protection around us, but only if we live the Christian life. The Christian life is not just the sinner's prayer, but a radical change in how one thinks, acts, and believes. This is a journey that has many bumps in the road, but one worth pursuing. Conversely, if God is not changing you, he is not saving you! Thus, if you're not saved, you're not a child of God.

Although life is difficult, God is with us. Further, all Christians have the Holy Spirit residing inside them. This is the third person within the Trinity. The Holy Spirit is not some mysterious force that comes and goes. Instead, he is a real being that you can lean on during difficult times. Granted, we cry out to Jesus during difficult periods in our lives, but it's the Holy Spirit that changes how we feel, think, and discern matters. Likewise, the strength of the Holy Spirit inside us is determined by our willingness to yield to him. So some Christians are indwelled by the fire of the Holy Spirit, whereas many other believers show no signs of his presence.

The church must realize Satan and his demons know their time is short. As a result, Satan is attacking mankind with a sense of urgency. He is deploying every tactic at his disposal. Technology is his latest device. Satan is using technology to deceive people with imagery, which dents their spiritual senses. This is noticeable in children and young adults today. Because in many ways, they are being brainwashed by the messages and imagery shown on their devices. Also, many are falling victim to oppressive spirits, which are controlling them.

Like all snares of the devil, Christians must exercise discernment in how they use technology. Technology is neither evil nor good, but a tool. Also, smartphones cannot be your idol. In short, it cannot be an item that controls you. Instead, it's just a tool that helps you with daily tasks. So if you are constantly concerned about your Facebook, Twitter, or email accounts on your phone it's controlling you. If so, realize Satan is using that device to distract you and keep your focus off God.

Despite this new tactic by Satan to deceive the world, believers have the authority in Jesus's name to discern and confront demonic forces. We confront demonic forces with the Word. In short, understanding how Scripture applies to a situation. In 2 Timothy 1:7 is a short but powerful verse to cite when fear comes up: **For God has not given us the spirit of fear; but of power, and of love, and of a sound mind.**

Yet if one does not believe the Bible is God's Word, citing Scripture won't deliver them from their plight. So one must develop faith in the Word. The Bible tells us that faith comes by hearing and by hearing the Word of God. Given this, if you want to know God and be delivered from demonic afflictions saturate yourself in the Word and refuse to accept the things of the devil.

Scripture Template

Every Christian has their favorite verses they dwell on during difficult times. Further, it's not necessary to cite Scripture verbatim. God knows the intent and faith we have in His Word. Given this, here are some Scripture segments to cite during difficult times:

- "I can do all things through Christ who strengthens me."(Phil. 4:13)
- "If God is for you, who can be against you." (Rom. 8:31)
- "Resist the Devil, and he will flee from you." (James 4:7)
- "Greater is he, who is in me, then he, who is in the world."(1 John 4:4)
- "We cannot even imagine the love God has for those that love him." (1 Cor. 2:9)
- "Every thought is captive; every spirit is tested." (1 John4:1)
- "Seek first the kingdom of God, and all these things will be added." (Matt. 6:33)
- "No good thing will God withhold from those who love him." (Ps. 84:11)
- "If I am obedient, I will eat the fruit of the lamb." (Isa.1:19)
- "The steps of a righteous man are ordered by God." (Ps.37:23)
- "The Lord will never allow the righteous man to stumble." (Prov. 10:29)
- "When I am weak, then I am strong." (2 Cor. 12:9–11)

- "It is not I that live, but Christ who lives in me." (Gal.2:20)
- "We cannot even imagine the blessings of those that love and fear the Lord." (1 Cor. 2:9)

- Nothing formed against me can stand." (Isa. 54:17)
- "There is a season for all things." (Eccles. 3:1)
- "I do not have a spirit of fear, but of power, love, and sound mind." (2 Tim. 1:7)
- "If you draw closer to me, I will draw closer to you."(James 4:18)

SALVATION VERSES

"For God so loved the world that He gave His only begotten Son, that whoever believes in Him should not perish but have everlasting life." (John 3:16)

That if you confess with mouth the Lord Jesus and believe in your heart that God has raised Him from the dead, you will be saved. For with the heart one believes unto righteous, and with the mouth confession is made unto salvation. (Rom. 10:9–10)

For the wages of sin is death, but the gift of God is eternal life in Christ Jesus our Lord. (Rom. 6:23)

Jesus answered and said to him, "Most assuredly, I say to you, unless one is born again, he cannot see the kingdom of God." (John 3:3)

"Not everyone who says to Me, 'Lord, Lord,' shall enter the kingdom of heaven, but he who does the will of My Father in heaven. (Matt. 7:21)

"I am the door. If anyone enters by Me, he will be saved, and will go in and out and find pasture." (John 10:9)

Jesus said to him, "I am the way, the truth, and the life. No one comes to the Father except through Me." (John 14:6)

Made in the USA
Columbia, SC
24 April 2025

56920063R00052